D'YOU HEAR THERE!

IN MEMORY
This book is dedicated to Commander Amy Gilmore MBE Royal Navy who sadly passed away in July 2025 after a battle with cancer, fought with fortitude, grace and humour. Amy and her husband Steve are an inspiration, and some of the proceeds of this book will be given to one of the charities which helped Amy and others, namely Weldmar Hospicecare.

Notwithstanding my pride to have known them both, I nevertheless recognize that Naval Aviators and Weapon Engineers are the butt of many of my quips in this book!! You pick your Branch Amy and Steve!

AUTHOR'S NOTE
I have, and always will have, a great feeling of loyalty towards my Service, and in particular a place in my heart for Devonport and Torpoint: an area of the UK in which I served so frequently and happily. Two other charities are therefore also recipients of some of the proceeds from this book: the Royal Naval Association and the China Fleet Country Club.

In purchasing this book you will also be helping others, and for that, above all, I thank you.

D'YOU HEAR THERE!

DAILY PIPES
OF THE
ROYAL NAVY

RICHARD HARRIS

Illustrations by Jim Nisbet

OSPREY PUBLISHING
Bloomsbury Publishing Plc

Kemp House, Chawley Park, Cumnor Hill, Oxford OX2 9PH, UK
Bloomsbury Publishing Ireland Limited,
29 Earlsfort Terrace, Dublin 2, D02 AY28, Ireland
Bloomsbury Publishing Inc.
1359 Broadway, 12th Floor, New York, NY 10018, USA
E-mail: info@ospreypublishing.com
www.ospreypublishing.com

OSPREY is a trademark of Osprey Publishing Ltd

First published in Great Britain in 2026

© Richard Harris, 2026

Richard Harris has asserted his right under the Copyright, Designs and Patents Act, 1988, to be identified as Author of this work.

All rights reserved. No part of this publication may be: i) reproduced or transmitted in any form, electronic or mechanical, including photocopying, recording or by means of any information storage or retrieval system without prior permission in writing from the publishers; or ii) used or reproduced in any way for the training, development or operation of artificial intelligence (AI) technologies, including generative AI technologies. The rights holders expressly reserve this publication from the text and data mining exception as per Article 4(3) of the Digital Single Market Directive (EU) 2019/790

A catalogue record for this book is available from the British Library.

ISBN: HB 9781472876188;
eBook 9781472876195;
ePDF 9781472876171;
XML 9781472876157;
Audio 9781472876164

26 27 28 29 30   10 9 8 7 6 5 4 3 2 1

Cover design by Stewart Larking
Index by Fionbar Lyons
Typeset by Lumina Datamatics Ltd
Printed and bound in Great Britain by Clays Ltd, Elcograf S.p.A.

Osprey Publishing supports the Woodland Trust, the UK's leading woodland conservation charity.

To find out more about our authors and books visit www.ospreypublishing.com. Here you will find extracts, author interviews, details of forthcoming events and the option to sign up for our newsletter.

For product safety related questions contact productsafety@bloomsbury.com

CONTENTS

Foreword	6
Preface	7
Day 1 – Harbour Hassle	13
Day 2 – A Day Alongside is a Day Wasted	40
Day 3 – FOST are Here to Help!	49
Day 45 – Hold On (Literally), the Heads are Out of Action	58
Day 46 – What is a Flight Deck Actually for Anyway?	69
Day 47 – Never Run Out of Beer … or Loo Rolls	87
Day 48 – Giblets and Haggis	99
Day 49 – Peg Me Out Shipmate!	108
Ghost Pipes	124
Acknowledgements	135
Glossary	136
Index	140

Foreword

Rich and I first met as fellow Logisticians in the Navy. Both of us started our naval careers at Torpoint, with Rich joining HMS *Raleigh* as an able seaman in the Royal Navy (RN) Reserves and me across the road at HMS *Fisgard* as a Tiffy Apprentice. Rich very kindly invited me to be his first Guest of Honour to take the salute at the Passing Out Parade during his tenure as the Captain of HMS *Raleigh*. It was a huge honour and allowed me to say to the passing out class that I would be happy to swap uniforms with any of them and start all over again – I know that Rich felt the same. It was clear that he loved serving there and took a keen interest in the lives of his staff and the recruits in his care. *Raleigh* flourished during his time.

I followed Rich's pipes when they were first posted on his social media profile as he travelled to and from London. They captured perfectly and accurately the actual pipes themselves and then unpacked aspects of those pipes, often with much humour, and, consequently, sparked recollections of time at sea which any matelot will share to some degree.

I am delighted that they have now been formally published, and am equally delighted, and touched, that Rich has kindly donated some of the proceeds of the sales to Service-related charities, including the Royal Naval Association. It is fitting, and typical, that an officer who commanded *Raleigh* with such an engaging touch has contributed not only to the start of sailors' careers but into their lives beyond the Service. I hope these pipes make you smile in the same way as they do for me.

Bill Oliphant
CEO The Royal Naval Association
Captain, Royal Navy, Retired

Preface

'Ahoy, me hearty!'

The unfailingly kind and optimistic but incredibly hard-working Capt Paul Burke RN greeted me as I walked to my desk on a Thursday morning. He was a submariner, battle hardened at sea and in the Ministry of Defence (MOD); his mariner's greeting made me smile at the start of an inevitably challenging day on the fifth floor of MOD in Whitehall. My Tube journey to work was a metaphorical thousand miles from my life at sea, and I often wished I was back there.

Shortly after I had opened my inbox, an officer from the Air Staff sidled up to my desk with an offer of coffee. On the eve of another Defence Review, very few people were truly one's friend in the MOD, even those from my own Service. The squadron leader's offer of coffee probably meant he was fishing for something from me; I would have done the same, and often did. As we chatted, another fellow naval commander arrived on the floorplate.

'Morning Shipmate!' he cried in his strong Geordie accent.

The young squadron leader enquired, 'Why is he calling you shipmate? You aren't on a ship!'

I sighed, and explained that the Navy has customs, traditions and its own language whereas the RAF has habits, and they are all bad! He chuckled and disappeared back to his desk.

He had a point, though. I was not on a ship, and neither the fellow commander nor Capt Burke and I had ever served together at sea. However, we shared a language, a tradition and unique seagoing experiences which meant that, whether serving at sea or ashore, we always proudly considered ourselves as sailors in the Royal Navy. We would go 'ashore' for a drink in Whitehall, we would make a 'wet' (i.e. a cup of tea/coffee) at 1030, we would have 'scran' at lunchtime, and if we were telling an almost unbelievable 'dit' (story) we would verify its truth by saying the word 'safeguard'". The very utterance of the word 'safeguard' would immediately inform the listener that this dit was true; it would also, very fleetingly, cast one's mind back to life at sea.

Some 220 miles to the west, a Type 23 frigate had just sailed south past the breakwater in Plymouth Sound. Earlier that day, painfully early for many, on the Bridge of the frigate, a sailor (the Bosun's Mate) had announced on the ship's main broadcast, 'D'you hear there ... the safeguard rule is now in force.' Everyone heard it, and everyone listened despite the fact that broadcaster was the most junior sailor onboard. It would be many hours until she announced, 'D'you hear there ... the safeguard rule is no longer in force.'

The sailor's main broadcast announcement, or any main broadcast announcement, is known in the Royal Navy as a 'pipe'. Every day, in a ship or a submarine or shore establishment, many pipes are made. The pipes will serve a number of purposes: they might inform the ship's company (i.e. the crew) that something important is about to happen (or has just happened); they might require certain sailors to go to a certain part of the ship; they might tell sailors to wake up or go to bed; they might tell sailors they are going to war; they might tell the sailors that they are no longer going to Barbados but are en route to the Falkland Islands instead; they might tell sailors that the heads (toilets) are not serviceable; they might alert people to a fire; they might even call sailors to prayer.

---

* During a ship's daily routine it will undertake a range of exercises to ensure the ship's company maintains its currency in responding to safety-related events. Each one of those exercises is piped with a prefix, e.g. 'For exercise, for exercise, for exercise ... fire, fire, fire, fire in the Galley'. If, however, during the course of the exercise, a real event occurs, a Pipe will be made with another prefix e.g. 'Safeguard, safeguard, safeguard, fire, fire, fire, fire in the After Engine Room'. This means that there really is a fire in the After Engine Room. Hence, 'safeguard' means 'I am telling the truth'!

PREFACE

In a ship and a submarine, daily pipes are a part of life. They are vital.

The following week, unusually, my duties required me to visit Her (late) Majesty's Dockyard in Devonport, Plymouth. I stayed in the Wardroom in HMS *Drake*. An old, grand building, it overlooked the Royal Dockyard and the ships and submarines which were berthed alongside there. Further across the River Hamoaze to the west lay the small Cornish town of Torpoint and the training establishment HMS *Raleigh*: the starting point of so many sailors' careers. Those sailors' first morning in the Navy will have been heralded by a pipe telling them to wake up.

That night my bedroom was, in fact, my cabin. As luck would have it, I was accommodated in the same cabin which I had occupied one night in September 1999 when, as a young lieutenant, I prepared to join the Type 23 frigate HMS *Somerset*. The cabin had not changed much in the ensuing 17 years. It still had an old basin, and the heads and bathrooms were a short walk, in flip flops, down the corridor. I thought it would be a grim night's sleep, but I had already begun to reminisce about my time at sea. I was pleased to learn that breakfast finished at 0830, so I looked forward to a lie in the following day.

Throughout the night, the ships lay silent in the dockyard, and all were awoken at 0700 by the shrill whistle of the Bosun's Call. It was the pipe 'Call the Hands'. On each ship's flight deck – situated on the upper deck, outdoors and therefore cold and wet – a sailor, who had spent the previous three hours trying to keep warm and dry as he guarded the ship at the top of the Gangway while his shipmates slept or returned from a night out, took some pleasure in making the pipe 'Call the Hands'. The pipe (i.e. a sharp whistle) pierced the air inside the ships and across the dockyard, and it woke both the sailors and some of the local neighbouring residents to the sound 'da da da da ... da da da daaaaaa, da da da da, da da da daaaaa ... da da da da ... da da da drrrrr, drrrrr, drrrrr'. The hands (the sailors) had indeed been called to wake up; hence 'Call the Hands'!

As I lay in the warmth of my cabin, I thought of the sailors stirring in those ships.

Then, at 0701, I heard the pipe from one of the ships, 'Officer of the Day, Visitor, Gangway', and I thought of an Officer of the Day (OOD), the duty officer for 24 hours, who was probably either in the shower or shaving, but who now had to quickly get changed and make their way to the Gangway to greet a visitor (for that is what the pipe meant). If one were being less pithy, one might otherwise announce, 'Please can the Officer of the Day come to the Gangway in order to meet a visitor.' However, this is the Royal Navy, and there is rarely the opportunity for courtesy in pipes, hence 'Officer of the Day, Visitor, Gangway'! Indeed, in many respects, the pipe is an order. One might ponder who wanted to see the OOD at 0701; it is likely that it is a member of the local constabulary.

At 0745 I heard another pipe: 'Leading Seaman Palmer, Regulating Office'. Literally translated, this pipe was telling Leading Seaman Palmer to report to the Regulating Office, the workplace of the Master at Arms (MAA), namely the ship's policeman or policewoman. This was almost certainly not a good pipe for Leading Seaman Palmer, and probably had something to do with the OOD's earlier discussion with the 'visitor' at the Gangway. The rest of Leading Seaman Palmer's shipmates would have heard this pipe, and all would be wondering what he might have done to earn the early morning call with the MAA.

For a moment I felt as if I was back at sea, and, as I made my way back to London later that day, I reflected and smiled to myself on the various pipes I had heard during my career; what they meant; what images they conjured up in my mind; and the various stories that emerged from the scenarios heralded by each pipe.

This book aims to take you onboard a warship; it matters little whether it is a modern warship or one that guarded our island 50 years ago. The language is invariably the same, as are the sailors and the lives they lead at sea. Modern communication or slavish gazing at phones or tablets has not overtaken the basic requirement for an occasional short verbal announcement to muster the collective effort of a group of sailors; hence these pipes are not only history, they are a small insight into how the Royal Navy still operates today.

They are deliberately humorous, and that reflects the fact that life at sea, despite its challenges, separation and professionalism, is laced, necessarily, with humour.

The translations are accurate. The associated anecdotes (or dits) are predominantly reflections from my career but reflect the Navy's principles that one 'never lets the truth get in the way of a good dit'! In 2017 I shared these pipes daily on social media during my Tube journeys to London, and it soon became clear that, although they were my reflections, many of my serving and veteran colleagues shared very similar experiences, and they raised a smile or prompted another anecdote. This subsequently gave me confidence that this book might, momentarily, take a sailor back to their life at sea, or indeed provide an insight into a sailor's life afloat for the benefit of friends and families.

Although perhaps a little grand, the pipes that you are about to read are a little bit of Royal Naval heritage. I hope they muster a smile, and also hope that the sales of this book add much-needed funds for some of our vital Service charities.

Richard Harris
September 2025

Day 1

Harbour Hassle

LOCATION: HIS MAJESTY'S NAVAL BASE DEVONPORT

'Call the hands, call the hands, call the hands.'
Unlike all of the other pipes in this book, technically this is a pipe that does not need to be spoken but is conveyed as a shrill, piercing whistle using a Bosun's Call. However, there are times when it is followed by the words 'Call the hands, call the hands, call the hands'.

The pipe is made by the Quartermaster (QM) or the Bosun's Mate (BM) on the Bridge or at the Gangway depending on whether the ship is at sea or alongside (i.e. in harbour). At Britannia Naval College (BRNC) Dartmouth, officers used to be taught to make this pipe (despite never needing to do it again in their career (a bit like flashing light communications or making an ornamental rockery)) and, if they were on duty, they would have to pipe it over the College's main broadcast.

'Call the Hands' (CTH) means that it is time to wake up. It is usually piped at 0700. During Operational Sea Training (OST) it is piped at 0300 allowing for a whole two hours 'in it' (i.e. in bed) having been up all night scrubbing out (i.e. cleaning the ship).

The ship will stir into life at this point. Some members of the ship's company will already be awake, namely those on watch, the chefs, those on camp beds in electronic distribution centres (EDCs)* and occasionally the Officer of the Watch (OOW) if the ship is at sea. The 90 per cent of the ship's company without washbasins in their

---

* Invariably there will be a greater demand for bunks than actually exist. This requires the use of camp beds in normal working compartments such as radar offices, or the Bomb Shop in a submarine.

accommodation will take their dhobey kit (washbag), wrap themselves in a towel and slip or slide up a ladder wearing flip flops to the nearest heads and bathrooms. If the accommodation is below the waterline it is possible that the access to the accommodation is through a kidney hatch built wide enough for a small person. This causes problems with respect to protecting one's privacy and dignity from time to time.

A glorious moment of being on watch overnight is the time when one goes to wake one's relief. While a Himalayan Sherpa guide or tracker dog would be of great use in finding one's relief in the dark, slightly smelly and snore-laden messdecks, the alternative option is to use the map in each messdeck showing who sleeps where, usually a laminated card with sailors' names scribbled in chinagraph pen or crayon. This is not necessarily an accurate reflection and tends to lead to the wrong person being woken up and having a torch shone in their face and being told, 'Oh, sorry shipmate, wrong bunk.' Having been wrongly woken, they will have managed to get back to sleep 5 minutes before CTH.

If the ship is at sea CTH will still be piped. The OOW will have followed the CTH pipe by greeting the ship's company with an occasionally witty morning sitrep (situation report, or update). This might provide meteorological updates, *Navy Day by Day*[*] updates or even a 'Happy Birthday' for a member of the ship's company. Many people either can't hear what the OOW is saying or may not actually care. Most will be smoking (known as tabbing) on the quarterdeck[†] where the sound of the propulsion and machinery may make most pipes inaudible. Those celebrating their birthday in a watch routine might be allowed 'all night in' having watched a film in the mess.

In days gone by, the communal gathering to watch a film in the mess was a treat, and as recently as when I joined the Navy (nearly 30 years ago) we would watch movies on projectors where the reel was changed half-way through, accompanied by ice cream or choc ice from the Navy, Army and Air Force Institutes (NAAFI) shop. Today, though, people can retire to their cabin or bunk space to watch a film on their tablet.

---

[*] This is a popular hardback book providing a history of the RN day by day.
[†] The quarterdeck on frigates and destroyers is at the very stern of a ship and is semi-exposed to the elements. The wake of the ship can be incredibly noisy when the ship is proceeding at best speed (fast).

On certain days, CTH will be piped later in the day or not at all. On a Daily Working Routine (when everyone works), CTH will be at 0700. On a Saturday Routine (when everyone works until 1200), CTH will be at 0700. On a Sunday Routine (when everyone works off their hangover until 0900), CTH is at 0800. On a Lazy Sunday Routine (when no-one works except the duty watch and the chefs), CTH is not piped at all. Some people never actually move from their beds on such days. There is such a thing as a Reverse Saturday Routine when CTH is piped at 1200 and people have the forenoon off (except the chefs).

'D'you hear there, 15 minutes to Colours, ratings as detailed on Daily Orders close up.'

This pipe is directing nominated personnel to proceed to the flightdeck (or the casing of a submarine, or the upper deck of a minor war vessel)* to report to the aft or bow of the ship or submarine, ready to hoist or lower the White Ensign and Union Flag respectively. It will usually be piped 15 minutes before Colours (usually 0800) and again 15 minutes before Sunset or Evening Colours.

The ceremony of Colours is when the Royal Navy's White Ensign is raised at the start of the day while alongside. The Union Flag is simultaneously hoisted or lowered at the bow of the ship. At the end of the day, the ceremony to lower the White Ensign and Union Flag is known either as Sunset, if it takes place at actual sunset, or as Evening Colours, which takes place at 2100 if actual sunset occurs later. The ceremony may also respectfully be known as 'putting the King/Queen to bed'.

It is a masterpiece of coordination, but a ceremony filled with risk. The Colour Party is made up of:

a sailor to raise the White Ensign
a sailor to pipe the 'Still'
a sailor to ring the bell

---

* Outside of the ship's superstructure.

a sailor to hoist the Union Flag
a sailor to raise and lower the Prep*
a sailor to make the pipe over the main broadcast
the OOD to give the orders

The Colour Party will be given a 15-minute warning pipe, reminding them, in accordance with Daily Orders, that the sun has once again risen (unless in Devonport or Faslane), and that they will be required to be present at 0745 in order to conduct Colours. Sadly, at least one member of the Colour Party might be adrift (late), and occasionally that might be the OOD.

Sometimes the OOD will hold a telescope under their port armpit, in case the French or Spanish Fleet should be sighted.

The telescope serves a practical purpose although it is rarely used. In base port, when performing the ceremony of Colours and Sunset each ship takes its lead from the senior ship enabling dockyard-wide coordination.† This requires the duty Communications Rating to spot the Prep (i.e. a flag) of the senior ship. If the rating cannot see the senior ship's Prep, they will make it up (i.e. look at their watch). Typically, if the ship has dared to conduct Colours before the senior ship, the OOD will be piped to take a shore telephone call from the senior ship. Alternatively, the senior ship might pen a signal. This makes the Executive Officer (XO) sad. Unless the Commanding Officer (CO)‡ is heavily 'pregnant' (expecting to be promoted), they are unlikely to care.

The evolution, as the ceremony is known, will typically proceed as follows:

Communications Rating (having spotted the Prep of the senior ship being raised and lowered) at 0759: *One minute to Colours, Sir/Ma'am/Chief!*

---

* The Preparatory Pennant – a flag used to initiate the sequence of Colours/Sunset.
† This reflects how ships used to communicate at sea in days of sail or even in the early days of steam, namely by flag, or latterly by flashing light.
‡ Usually known as 'The Captain'.

OOD: *Very good!*

The OOD will then count to 20 (in their head), and bring the Colour Party to attention: *Colour Party, ho!*

Communications Rating (having spotted the Prep of the senior ship being lowered 'at the dip'[*]) at 0800: *Colours, Sir/Ma'am/Chief!*

OOD: *Make it so!*

At this point another rating, whose job it is to ring the bell, will give eight rings of the bell, or maybe six or seven (for no good reason), or none at all, causing the OOD again to shout:

Make it so!

The bell will sound as follows: DING DING-DING DING-DING DING-DING DING

OOD: *Pipe the Still!*

The BM will then pipe the Bosun's Call for 8 seconds (i.e. the Still).
 The QM will pipe over the ship's main broadcast: **'Attention on the upper deck, face aft and salute, Colours.'**[†]
 At this point, the White Ensign will be hoisted. The same procedure is applied to the lowering of the White Ensign at Sunset or Evening Colours, except that a bell is not rung.
 Once the White Ensign has been hoisted and the Prep has been lowered, this will signify the end of the ceremony.
 The Colour Party will be ordered as follows:

OOD: *Colour Party, turning left and right, dissssss-misss.* This will confuse the sailors, causing them to turn in various random directions.

---

[*] This is when the Prep is partially lowered (but not fully lowered).
[†] Or 'Sunset' or 'Evening Colours' as appropriate.

HARBOUR HASSLE

Once Colours is complete the QM will pipe: **'Out pipes, duty part of the watch Fire and Emergency Party, both watches of the Warfare department, muster oooooonnnnn[*] the flight deck.'**

This pipe is telling certain personnel that they are to muster on the flight deck at the start of the working day. At that point, the OOD and the duty senior rate will gather the Fire and Emergency Party (the small team charged with the safety of the ship for the next 24 hours) on the flight deck (or sweep deck or PAP deck on minesweepers and hunters respectively, or hangar on an aircraft carrier). The junior ratings will each be given a coloured surcoat denoting their particular fire and emergency party role for the period of their watch. Incidentally, the wording 'Out pipes' is a nod to days gone by when sailors were to extinguish their pipes and 'turn to', namely to start working.

Concurrently, the Warfare department, split into Port and Starboard Watches, will also muster to discuss which parts of the ship will be cleaned, scrubbed and painted during the day. They may also rig an awning for a cocktail party or ship's reception.

The other departments do not muster in this manner as it is obvious to them what their job is (mainly due to a higher NAMET[†] score, and being slightly cleverer! (see page 66)).

After a very good run ashore it is possible that a less than comprehensive muster will occur, because some personnel either are still ashore or are in their rack/cart/scratcher (slang for asleep). This is likely to lead to a pipe directing a sailor to the Regulating Office.

---

[*] Occasionally the word 'on' will be lengthened for no apparent reason.
[†] Naval Maths and English Test. This is a test undertaken by all RN ratings to establish aptitude to serve in certain branches of the RN, as well as being a qualification for promotion. The naming of the test changes over time (e.g. NAMET, LANTERN etc.).

'D'you hear there, the following personnel muster at the Regulating Office: Writer Cleary, RO White and Leading Seaman Palmer. Those personnel muster at the Regulating Office.'

At least six personnel will be sad to hear this pipe: Writer Cleary[*], Radio Operator (RO) White and Leading Seaman Palmer, as well as their divisional officers (DOs), namely their line managers.

If one of these individuals was supposed to be at the muster of both watches, but was adrift, then this is a potential reason for being required to visit the Regulating Office!

The summons to the Regulating Office is likely to be an early stage of an investigation into a misdemeanour with which the three personnel have been associated (and whose guilt is assumed by most, if not all, members of the ship's company). Having been thoroughly investigated[†] by the MAA, with an appropriate messdeck sweepstake undertaken to guess the punishment, the ratings will appear in front

---

[*] Pay, administration and correspondence staff are known as Writers.
[†] Not necessarily thoroughly.

of the XO or the Captain's Table (depending upon the gravity of the crime) for a summary hearing.* The DO will be required to provide mitigation. If the DO cannot concoct a suitable excuse for why the rating committed the crime, at the very least they might say that the rating works hard and does not have any money, in order to trigger a degree of clemency from the XO or CO.

The DO can, of course, tell the truth as to what happened, as in the case of Able Seaman (AB) Bell who went Absent Without Leave (AWOL) to an exotic bar while on a run ashore in Rio. When AB Bell finally returned onboard, and the Captain asked the DO at his Table why Bell was adrift, the DO said, 'Well, it was just Rio, Sir, what more can I say?' The Captain was displeased with this reason (I recall standing behind the Captain at the time and watching him becoming enraged).

Being a DO is a weighty responsibility especially if one is a DO for a chef or a stoker (a Marine Engineer, or ME). Being a DO for a Writer is usually less challenging, although there was one occasion when a young Writer had cause to appear at the Captain's Table for drunkenness. When asked by the Captain whether there was any mitigation, the DO replied, 'Well, Sir, he was drinking with the chefs.'

The Writer was admonished and told to put it down to experience.

On another occasion, which as the DO I witnessed personally, another Leading Writer collapsed midway through a very important pipe which *should* have proceeded as follows: **'D'you hear there, diving is taking place on the ship's hull. Gash is not to be ditched. No underwater equipment is to be started or stopped without first contacting the SCC.'**

This pipe is informing people that rudders, shafts, sonars and rubbish waste (gash) cannot be ditched overboard because of the presence of divers examining the ship's hull, and that the Ship's Control Centre (SCC) should be contacted before starting or

---

* A visit to the Captain's Table does not involve a meal (we are not talking about Captain Birdseye here!).

stopping underwater equipment. It is a very important, safety-critical pipe.

Sadly, on the occasion of the incident highlighted above, while the ship was alongside in Tenerife, the Leading Writer had had a late night ashore with the chefs, and he was the HQ1 watchkeeper[*]. Unfortunately, he only managed to utter this pipe up to the word 'hull', and then lost the ability to speak. He was subsequently disrated (demoted) and I could offer little in mitigation, not least because he was always ashore with the chefs.

'Chef Knowles, pizza, Gangway.'

This appears to be a fairly straightforward pipe unless the ship is at sea (which has happened on occasion). The pipe informs the recipient that a pizza delivery has arrived at the bottom of the Gangway. It is worrying if a chef has ordered it, especially before evening scran[†], and even more especially if the chef is on duty given that they will have made the evening meal.

Obtaining a vehicle pass to gain entry (e.g. for a pizza delivery) into one of His Majesty's dockyards can be a challenge irrespective of whether one is a member of the Armed Forces or a civilian. Most Naval personnel will spend several hours of their careers attempting to obtain a car permit to enter a dockyard. It involves endless queuing, photographs (despite having a photographic Armed Forces ID card), and usually watching a Health and Safety video (despite undergoing annual Health and Safety training). One of the videos used to advise sailors not to feed toxic waste to gulls (which therefore suggests this probably happened on one occasion). To add insult to injury, contractors and non-military visitors to the dockyard will undergo the same process, but will be processed quicker! Unfortunately all

---

[*] The HQ1 watchkeeper is usually a leading hand charged with being the first point of contact in the event of making the ship's company aware of an emergency or any proactive safety-based announcements.

[†] Breakfast, lunch or dinner.

of HM dockyards have completely different entry procedures, and do not share car information. Usually a sailor will arrive at their next ship late in the evening, having travelled from another dockyard or from leave during the day. Arriving in 'the silent hours' (i.e. not during the standard working day), they will be given a temporary permit which will expire at 0700 the following day, meaning that they will probably have to get up at 0630, waking their new mess mates in the process, to drive back to the Pass Office to obtain a permanent pass. The Pass Office may well be closed.

The CO and XO might have the privilege of being able to park their cars close to the ship. The rest of the ship's company are rarely so lucky, and they can typically park three miles away. Occasionally, the lucky few heads of department are also able to park their cars on the jetty next to the ship. This is a privilege, but it is fraught with risk. For example, one must take care if the ship is due to sail out into the middle of the dockyard waters temporarily in order to visit the ammunitioning buoys, which puts it technically at sea. Once ammunitioning is complete, the ship will usually be told to berth at the other end of the dockyard from its berth at the start of the day. By this time, personnel who parked next to the ship will have had a parking ticket placed on the windscreen as they are technically no longer eligible to be parked there – which will have since stuck to the window given the torrential rain. Fortunately, the traffic control authorities are always polite and sympathetic.

'Attention on the upper deck, face to port, HMS *Fearless.*'

This pipe is informing members of the ship's company who are on the upper deck, or about to proceed onto the upper deck, that the ship is about to be passed by another ship, and therefore a short ceremonial procedure will take place that effectively requires everyone on the upper deck to stand to attention (which most people find to be an irritation). Thus, those personnel who were about to proceed onto the upper deck will probably delay doing so unless they are the OOD! Alternatively, some personnel who are on the upper deck will run for the nearest hatch or door so that they do not have to stand to attention for 30 seconds!

The OOD should have read the Movements Signal at the beginning of their 24-hour duty. This will tell the OOD which ships are moving around the dockyard, if diving is taking place or if there are senior officers afloat (sporting a variety of boat discs[*] depending on what formality they wish to apply). Incidentally, the displaying of boat discs was always a good Young Officer Fleetboard[†] question, although to this day I do not recall seeing any discs being displayed and never received a signal expressing disappointment. The OOD will determine which is the senior ship and which is the junior ship by consulting the Bridge Card. The Bridge Card lists the name of every ship and submarine in the Royal Navy (RN), and the seniority of the CO of each vessel. It is the responsibility of the 'junior' ship to salute the 'senior' ship.

If the OOD is not particularly switched on, either they will not have read the Movements Signal or they will have forgotten it while undertaking the myriad of other duties of an OOD, such as distributing keys, conducting various emergency exercises, watching TV in the mess, eating, sleeping, taking draught marks, conducting rounds (inspections), checking the jetty, performing Colours and Sunset, taking a shore telephone call from the Gangway, certifying drunkenness, mustering crypto and mustering the safe. Having not noted the Movements Signal it is likely that the OOD either will miss saluting the passing ship altogether or will be seen rushing to the ship's side just as the other ship passes. If the OOD's ship is junior to the passing ship and either misses the occasion or performs the 'ceremonial' poorly, this will probably result in a 'disappointed' signal from the senior captain. Subsequently, the junior captain, having seen the signal on the Signals Board (containing reams of paper), will 'discuss' this with the OOD, but the discussion will have limited two-way dialogue. It may result in the OOD undertaking another

---

[*] A range of discs can be displayed by a boat indicating the type of formality expected by the senior officer in that boat.

[†] The YOFB – a key examination required for junior officers to continue their careers.

duty or being required to submit Reasons in Writing (which is a sophisticated way of doing 'lines' from one's school days!).

On one occasion, an unnamed CO* who, at that time, was the most junior CO in the RN, brought his ship back into Portsmouth Naval Base playing 'The Boys are Back in Town' over its main broadcast. He was invited to see his flotilla commander.†

The Royal Navy prides itself on its ceremonial duties. All officers of foreign navies are saluted when they board and disembark a British warship. This is an onerous duty for the Gangway staff who will have to 'pipe the side' while the CO and the XO stand to attention carrying a telescope (I don't know why). The OOD will titter or scowl over the standard of saluting by the different nationalities. Should a British Army officer board the ship, their salute is likely to cause a titter; should an RAF officer board the ship, their salute might struggle to produce a return salute!

'D'you hear there, anyone knowing the whereabouts of the Officer of the Day's keys, contact HQ1.'

Occasionally one might hear a pipe which will make one chuckle at another's misfortune. On this occasion it would appear that the OOD has lost their keys (not their car keys!). They will have almost certainly have looked everywhere for the keys before resorting to this pipe. If the OOD is lucky, the CO and XO will be ashore; the OOD would not wish them to know that the keys were missing. If the CO is ashore it is possible that the CO will have invited some officers to accompany them (and they will be wise to accept the offer).

The OOD's keys are important. There are several important keys in a ship; indeed the important keys are so important that they have their own pipe as well … 'Important Keys' (occasionally changed to 'Impotent Keys'). The OOD's keys contain keys to the OOD's

---

* Steve Dainton.
† His immediate superior officer.

safe and the Shiphaz Board. The Shiphaz Board is located on the Bridge and identifies certain parts of the ship or activities along with the particular pieces of equipment which need to be isolated (i.e. switched off) so that people are not injured.

The OOD's safe will be secured by keys and a combination. If only there was some way of remembering the combination code – such as an electric distribution marker on an adjacent bulkhead*?! When I was under training in HMS *Nottingham* I understudied a very experienced Chief Petty Officer (CPO) as OOD, and he said, 'Now, Sir, if you forget the combination number just walk around the corner and look at the EDC number on the bulkhead!'

The safe will contain a number of important items.

There will be a sum of money (sterling and local currency), typically used to pay off an irate taxi driver having returned an inebriated sailor to the ship (this will be recovered if (when) the sailor is found guilty of returning onboard drunk. The PO/CPOWTR[†] will have to work into the Dogs (i.e. after 1600) to input the deduction from the sailor's pay account).

Important documents will also be inside the safe, and they will guide the OOD on immediate actions such as when encountering a nuclear explosion in Devonport, or a sailor taking illegal drugs. The safe will house the Port Guide, enabling the OOD to access a range of telephone numbers they might need in an emergency.

The OOD's day of duty[‡] is challenging and long. It will commence with a handover from the offgoing OOD after Colours, and will be followed by mustering the duty watch Fire and Emergency Party (see page 19). During the next 24 hours these gallant sailors can expect to deal with some or all of the following: fire, flood, fuel spillage, an intruder, a collision, a casualty, a VIP, a drunk sailor, an arrival of bread and milk, a storm, Ship Open to Visitors, an unsecured gangway. The OOD will have undertaken an examination board to prove proficiency in dealing with all of these occurrences.

---

* Wall.
[†] Senior pay and cash administrator.
[‡] Conducted when the ship is alongside. It can also happen at sea, but is far less onerous.

HQ1 is the compartment in which the SCC is invariably also located. Many of the ship's emergencies are coordinated from the SCC, and the OOD can expect to lead the following 24 hours transiting between HQ1, the Gangway, the Bridge, the Galley, their mess and their cabin. The OOD can expect to be piped to the Gangway or HQ1 every 10 minutes. Two sharp pips on the Bosun's Call will indicate to the OOD that they are required at the Gangway immediately, possibly because the CO is in sight and about to return onboard. It may also mean that a very senior officer has also unexpectedly appeared in sight.

The OOD will muster the safe and crypto material. During the crypto muster the duty Communications Rating will rattle off meaningless letters and numbers to the OOD, who will pretend to tick corresponding items off a check list.

At various times of the day, the OOD will attend the Shiphaz Board to ensure that various dangerous items of equipment are isolated in order to enable sailors to work without being knocked out or 'cooked' (radiated) from the inside out.

The OOD should visit the Galley during meal times. This is to enable sailors to raise any complaints which might not have been satisfactorily addressed by the Killick Chef*. To my knowledge very few OODs ventured behind the serving counter, and very few complaints were elevated beyond the Killick Chef. When deployed abroad on a Lazy Sunday routine, the chefs might be required to cook brunch instead of the normal breakfast. This entails cooking every piece of meat known to man/woman, and chips, and it costs a lot of money despite the fact that most of the ship's company is either in bed or ashore. This therefore makes a significant dent into the catering account and makes the Caterer sad.

During the period of duty the OOD will have consulted the exercise log in order to determine which exercise should be conducted by the duty watch. The OOD will have been pleased to learn that it will be an instruction period for the duty watch, but less pleased to note that a head-of-department-covered fire exercise

---

* Senior chef of the watch.

(FIREX) will be taking place. The latter means that a major exercise will take place and will be overseen and umpired by one of the ship's heads of department. It therefore needs to be taken seriously. It also tends to mean that the exercise will require everyone onboard to take part in some shape or form. As a result, most of the ship's company will opt to go ashore before the exercise is likely to commence rather than help their shipmates who are on duty.

Having had four hours' sleep, the OOD will wearily proceed to the Gangway before Colours to determine if any sailors are adrift. The Gangway staff will briefly emerge from the slight warmth of the kaboosh[*] with only their noses sticking out of their greatcoats. During the duty, the OOD may have witnessed sailors returning from the run ashore, some singing, some staggering, some crying, some bleeding, some eating. They may even have had cause to lock up a sailor who was particularly worse for wear through drink. I did this once when OOD in HMS *Collingwood*[†], and when I released the sailor the following day I was alarmed to discover that the sailor was not even serving in HMS *Collingwood* but was a member of HMS *Newcastle*'s ship's company which was, at that time, in Newcastle.

Most notable incidents during my time as an OOD were as follows:

1. (As Second Officer of the Day (2OOD[‡])) Being asked to leave the Wardroom for eating a hamburger with my hands.
2. Wearing my ice cream suit[§] as the 'Ceremonial Officer of the Day' in Freetown, Sierra Leone, as gun shots were fired from ashore. The only other people allowed on the upper deck were the armed Deterrent Force. So, three armed personnel and a man in a bright white suit.
3. My first duty in Gibraltar. Never a quiet night.

---

[*] Temporary flimsy portacabin used to provide shelter for the Gangway staff.
[†] A shore establishment in Fareham, Hampshire.
[‡] The 2OOD is an understudy to the OOD (i.e. under training).
[§] Tropical white uniform.

HARBOUR HASSLE

4. As 2OOD on the same day as No. 1 (above) being asked to leave the Wardroom for eating a banana with my hands.

In any one working day alongside, the following pipes will be heard (number of times in brackets):

'Officer of the Day, Gangway' (14)
'Officer of the Day, HQ1' (20)
'Officer of the Day, shore telephone call, Gangway' (5)
'Officer of the Day, Shiphaz Board' (6) – note that this should ideally be an even number as whichever equipment has been isolated should, in theory, be deisolated at some stage (see page 96 ('Hands to Bathe'))
'Officer of the Day, visitor, Gangway' (7)
'Duty PO*, Gangway' (12)
'Duty PO, HQ1' (15)
'Duty ME Senior Rate, Gangway' (6)
'Duty ME Senior Rate, HQ1' (15)
'QM, Gangway' (0)†

'Bandit, bandit, bandit, intruder in the ship. RF to muster!'
This pipe means that an intruder has managed to break into the ship having successfully dodged the ever-vigilant Deterrent Force (DF), otherwise known as the QM, BM and Upper Deck Sentry or UDS; and the Response Force (RF) is now required to address this potentially serious issue.

There are all kinds of reasons why and how the intruder managed to evade the DF. They may have skilfully climbed a berthing rope avoiding the rat guards. They may have boarded via the quarterdeck, miraculously avoiding the tabbers (i.e. smokers). They might be a dockie‡ if it is between 0900 and 1200. Or, more likely, the UDS

---

* Duty petty officer.
† See Ghost Pipes (from page 124).
‡ Civilian dockyard worker.

was on the other side of the ship, the BM was making a wet and the QM was hunkered down avoiding the weather in the kaboosh. In HMNB Devonport, affectionately known as Guzz, the intruder may have gained entry to the dockyard under the guise of a taxi driver or pizza delivery person (see page 22).

With everyone alerted that an intruder is onboard, the members of the ship's company should go to a nearby compartment and lock themselves inside until further notice. For some, such as Weapon Engineers (WEs), the Executive Warrant Officer (EWO) and Battlestaff*, this is second nature.

Meanwhile, the RF (who also double as a firefighting team, first aid team and cleaning party) will proceed to the RF locker to be met by the Duty PO, who will provide them with their weapons and ammunition. The RF can comprise a range of personnel including Warfare Ratings, engineers and logisticians. They are all highly trained weapon handlers[†] … one of them might have shot a shark or sailor during 'Hands to Bathe'. I am unsure what the immediate action should have been if the intruder and RF coincidentally all went to the RF locker at the same time.

The OOD will have proceeded to HQ1 having shut the battered, fragile door to the compartment. This thin door will have a removable vent which can be removed by a small child.

Having arrived at HQ1 the OOD will now seek to engage with the intruder. The scripted pipe will be along the following lines: **'This is the Officer of the Day. I am addressing this to the person gaining entry to the ship. We know you are here and I have armed personnel searching for you. It is only a matter of time before you are found, and I would urge you to pick up the nearest phone and dial zero.'**

---

* If an admiral or commodore is embarked, the 'Battlestaff' is their planning staff.
† They are not!

There are some concerns and challenges presented by this pipe:

1. The intruder will not know what an OOD is (unless they have read this book or King's Regulations for the Royal Navy).
2. Having been undeterred by the DF, the intruder might not be afeared at the thought of a stoker, a Writer, a Greenie*, a Jack Dusty† and a dabber‡ in hot pursuit.
3. Ships' phones do not look like phones unless one is familiar with 'Space 1999'.
4. When 'foreign' (abroad), unless the OOD has used an interpreter or the ship's agent, the intruder is unlikely to understand the OOD unless they are fluent in English. I always thought it might be helpful to have a recorded message in another language (e.g. Arabic, American English, Welsh or Janner). I could have got a Herbert Lott award for that.§ Another reason for the lack of comprehension is because if the OOD is a dabber, they will shout through the microphone (rendering it muffled), or the main broadcast will be 'u/s' (broken). The duty communications equipment maintainer will be ashore or in bed – locked in their cabin.
5. Should the intruder dial zero it is not guaranteed that the HQ1 watchkeeper will answer the call promptly (see page 21).

Fortunately, if seeking to escape, helpful arrows will enable the intruder to find their way out.

'Daily Editorials!'
This pipe technically means that newspapers are available for purchase on the jetty. If a ship had been at sea for a number of weeks (particularly before online media) this would be a very welcome pipe.

---

* Weapon Engineer.
† Supply Chain Specialist.
‡ Warfare Officer or Rating.
§ This is an award given for an innovative idea.

The explanation of this pipe is very much based on days gone by (i.e. before online communication), although some facets explained below still exist.

In HM dockyards, the pipe would mean that actually a range of publications were available for purchase as well as newspapers. In Devonport the vendor once received a thank you letter from the well-known publisher Paul Raymond for being the biggest supplier of 'top-shelf' special interest publications in Plymouth.*

Before the days of internet, once at sea, news would be provided in the form of a signal from the UK providing a summary of the top stories. No pictures, just words. It was, therefore, a relatively dull way of keeping in touch with news from home and across the world. Ships' companies would eagerly await football results on a Saturday.

Having sailed, the range of newspapers and magazines in messes would become inevitably dated, but, in the absence of any other material, they would nonetheless be picked up for a cursory glance at some stage. Publications of last resort tended to be *The Naval Engineering Review* or *The Naval Review* and these were really only picked up after many weeks at sea. Occasionally such reading material would find its way into the heads (i.e. toilets) to provide topical reading for the occupant of the 'trap'. This was a welcome alternative to a flight safety cartoon attached to the bulkhead or an extract of *Rules of the Road*.

Visitors to the ship or new joiners while abroad would be treated with great contempt if they had failed to bring copies of the most recent newspapers from home. Officers, of course, only really read *The Times* or the *Telegraph*; publications such as *'The Currant Bun'* (*The Sun*) or the *Daily Mirror* might be frowned upon. This, incidentally, was a guaranteed question for those attending the officers' Admiralty Interview Board (AIB). One and a half days of examinations and leadership and planning exercises would culminate in a grilling by three panel members; usually a captain/colonel Royal Marines, commander and schoolmaster: *What newspaper do you read, Mr Davey?*

---

* Google Paul Raymond if unsure.

HARBOUR HASSLE

The Sun is not a welcome response; and if one were instead to answer *The Times* (purely for effect), one would strongly be advised to also gain a reasonable understanding of the typical contents of the newspaper for fear of being found out* when probed further.

Readers will wish to note the dual purpose of editorials (i.e. shin pads for deck hockey).

This pipe also brings the existence of signals to the reader's attention. Signals were, until the late 1990s/early 2000s, the primary method of providing swift written communication to and from a ship. They are still used. The challenge was, and still is, much greater for submarines to maintain their invariable covert posture. Signals would be, and still are, provided to the CO on a Signals Board on which they would see every signal sent to the ship in paper form. Other officers and key personnel would visit the Main Communication Office (MCO) to browse signals. Later, as technology allowed, personnel could read signals on a computerised DIMPS terminal. This terminal was the size of a small house, with a screen the size of a mobile telephone.

Other written correspondence would be received on or leave the ship by standard mail, and each seagoing unit would have its own British Forces Post Office (BFPO) number. The MOD Mail Centre at Mill Hill would be responsible for coordinating the movement of mail. If the ship's programme had suddenly changed (see page 60/61), among other things this might mean that mail or stores that had been originally sent to meet the ship in Kingston, Jamaica, might now have to find their way to Mare Harbour, Falkland Islands. These would be sad times, usually leading to delays in the receipt of mail, and a lack of synchronized mail. For example, one might read a letter stating that 'Sidney' (the dog) was buried yesterday, and a few weeks later receive a letter stating that Sidney had just died.

The arrival of mail would be a moment of excitement for many, and frustration that having received 40 bags of redirected mail, the

---

* This might be one of the reasons why I failed my first AIB. I did not know the name of the political editor.

Writers and Reggies* were taking an agonizingly long time to sort it. Eventually, the following pipe would be made: **'D'you hear there, mail is now ready for collection from the Ship's Office.'**

Among the eagerly awaited personal mail from family and friends would be newspapers, magazines and official mail. The Captain's mail would be processed by the Captain's Secretary or the Correspondence Officer (CORRO). The Captain's Secretary would be a junior Logistics or Supply and Secretariat (S&S) officer. The CORRO would be a junior Warfare/Seaman officer, probably in their first assignment. Accordingly, their primary focus would be Bridge watchkeeping and gaining their Watchkeeping Certification (also known as their 'ticket'). As a result, some CORROs neither liked nor were particularly capable of this role despite being trained in the infamous 'Office Simulator'. The Captain's Secretary, on the other hand, eagerly awaited the mail. It was not unusual for a CORRO to receive a bundle of official mail and immediately put it all into a bigger envelope and address it to their own ship so that it could be put back into the MOD's mail system, arrive at Mill Hill, and placed on an aircraft to meet the ship during the next port visit.

As well as receiving written correspondence, sailors would send letters home through the MOD Mail system (appending a British stamp from the NAAFI), or alternatively a postcard could be despatched from one of the exotic runs ashore. This might take many months to arrive home. There is a strong chance that the postcard might not ever be despatched. It might not even be written. Indeed, it might not even be purchased. However, that is not to say the intent to make the purchase was not there. This is otherwise known as a 'postcard run' or a 'haircut run'. What commenced as a quiet stroll into the local town to purchase a postcard or a haircut will be undone by stopping at one of the local bars in order to have a 'quiet one'. Invariably, these opportunities evolve into a fully blown run ashore. There are a number of consequences of a 'postcard/haircut' run.

---

* Regulators (Coppers).

A lack of correspondence home might be frowned upon. Additionally, the lack of a professional haircut might lead to the need to have one's hair cut onboard by one of the less proficient members of the ship's company. Although the ship's welfare fund may benefit from the payment, it may come at the cost of an unintended wedge into one's hairstyle or indeed a very short haircut. For ratings this might just be acceptable, but for officers it is likely to cause disappointment from the Captain. Indeed, the Captain might direct that the hairstyle is so poor that the officer should 'Remain Onboard' (ROB).

A ship's barber (not to be confused with King Neptune's Barber[*]), albeit a loose term, is one of several semi-private enterprises run by members of the ship's company. In submarines or smaller ships, members of the ship's company might volunteer to run a shop selling 'nutty'[†] and 'goffas'[‡]. In larger ships a much more sophisticated venture might be embarked upon, usually known as XXXX[§] Enterprises. So, for example, Chatham Enterprises will sell a range of items including polo shirts and baseball caps. Hence, if you find yourself onboard for Parent and Children at Sea (PACAS) and you hear, **'D'you hear there, Chatham Enterprises will be open on 1 Juliet Flat[¶] for the next 3 Zero minutes'**, this will be an opportunity to purchase a reminder of your time onboard a Pusser's Grey (i.e. an RN Warship).

'Jack Blair Menswear.'
This pipe is similar to 'Daily Editorials' in that it hints at what is meant but nonetheless seems slightly odd.

Many veteran readers will be aware of Jack Blair (a retailer of fairly modern clothing), and many will have used his services, though

---

[*] See from page 128.
[†] Confectionary.
[‡] Fizzy drinks.
[§] Insert the ship's name.
[¶] Area of internal deck.

few would wish to admit it. It is possible that in Phase 2 training establishments personnel may have actually been ordered to visit Jack Blair. Certainly, at BRNC officers were strongly encouraged to attend Gieves and Hawkes in order to obtain a proper cap and suitable attire (not denim) for proceeding ashore.

It is likely that during the 1980s and 1990s, the first store card possessed by a sailor or officer would be from one of these retailers, and they would often offer quite generous credit limits. The offer of a credit arrangement would enable sailors to pay for their items of stylish clothing without handing over their hard-earned cash; this enabled the cash to be retained for a run ashore down the 'Strip'*, or Emma's or Joanna's[†].

Many sailors would have purchased their first pair of dark navy Ron Hill leggings there, and the retailer was also the main supplier of Union Jack shorts to HM Fleet. As well as Jack Blair being 'now in attendance on the jetty', shops were located outside of Albert Gate in Devonport, Queen Street in Portsmouth and very close to the main gate of Portland dockyard.

A variety of items were available for purchase at Jack Blair including electronics and watches. These could be purchased and, in the event of a shortage of funds at a later stage, the items could be taken to Shaun's (or any other pawnbroker) for conversion to cash. Sailors are highly susceptible to the opportunity to purchase items and 'gizzits' (souvenirs or mementos of their time abroad), and were particularly fond of the Gully Gully Man[‡] during transits through the Suez Canal.

An alternative method of replenishing funds was to go on deployment and then blow the savings on a visit to Jack Blair upon one's return.

If a sailor was subsequently promoted to the upper deck (i.e. to the officer corps) they might have been encouraged to switch allegiance

---

* Union Street in Devonport.
† Nightclubs in Gosport and Southsea respectively.
‡ The Gully Gully Man was an entertainer and purveyor of fairly worthless items who would temporarily embark in HM ships during the slow passage through the Suez Canal.

to Louis Bernard. In such circumstances they could purchase a set of 'dog robbers' (jacket and tie) or 'planters' (casual shirt and trousers). The planters comprised either a powder blue shirt, or checked shirt, and beige chino trousers with brogues. In the days of a heightened domestic security threat, when personnel were strongly encouraged not to wear uniform ashore, it would nonetheless be easy to spot a member of the Royal Navy, either because of this typical civilian attire or because of ironed denim jeans, or because they were wearing a jacket in the middle of summer. That being said, I once wore my uniform for a journey from Plymouth to Portsmouth and when I stopped to purchase petrol the person behind the counter asked me, 'Who do you fly for?'

In many ways, officers who joined as Direct Graduate Entry Officers* (not necessarily bright), University Cadet Entry Officers† (annoyingly bright, and often just annoying) or Naval College Entry Officers‡ (assumed to be not very bright but were probably bright and just could not be bothered to study for a degree) were quite easy to distinguish from officers who were promoted from the lower deck as 'yardies' (ratings)§. Firstly, at BRNC they were usually more tired on account of knowing none of the tricks of the trade. Secondly, they were paid considerably less than yardies. Thirdly, they were less pub-fit (but became fit remarkably quickly). And finally, yardies insisted on wearing their waterproof flasher macs, or storm jackets, as well as Pusser's¶ caps rather than purchase these from Thieves and Sharks (Gieves and Hawkes). The Pusser's caps were very basic plastic-coated caps which were flat-topped and made the wearer look like Ernie (who drove the fastest milk cart in the west).

---

* Directly from university, usually as sub-lieutenants or, for some bizarre reason, if joining as an Education Officer (who typically would go to sea for a week during their career) they would join as a lieutenant.
† Join at the of 18 (or 12), undertake basic officer training and then go to university on full pay as a midshipman (middy).
‡ Join at the age of 18 (or 12) as a middy.
§ Senior Upperyardmen (SUY, previously known as Special Duties (SD) Officers) (very old) or Upperyardmen (UY) (not old).
¶ Uniform gratis issue.

Jack Blair no longer visits RN warships; time has moved on, although the clothing tastes of RN personnel have not. It is, therefore, a pipe that is no longer used, and would be out of place in today's Navy. That being said, even when Jack Blair was in existence, the pipe was still occasionally made out of place. In particular, during Damage Control training, when sailors are placed in a large steel hydraulically operated module in which flooding is simulated (and which is generally considered to be exceptionally realistic), the mood might be momentarily lightened by the pipe 'Jack Blair is now in attendance on the jetty'!

'D'you hear there, the following personnel have stores on the jetty: the Navigation Officer, Charge Chief Simpson, Chief Petty Officer Rhodes, Petty Officer Slater, Petty Officer Kershaw, LAEM Doubleday. Those personnel have stores to collect on the jetty.'

This pipe is informing some personnel that they have stores to collect from the jetty, and on this occasion the recipients range from a lieutenant (i.e. the Navigation Officer) to a Leading Air Engineering Mechanic (i.e. LAEM Doubleday).

The distribution and signing for stores is a sensitive subject. Jack Dusties believe that stores are purely for storing and not issuing. If stores are issued to individuals, unless the items are considered to be consumable, they are likely to require temporary custodians to sign for the stores on pain of death. The stores will be assigned to an individual's permanent loan record (PLR). These are required to be mustered on a six-monthly basis; it is a moment of great fear for the PLR holder, as if any item of stores is defective or missing it is likely to lead to a form being raised (C126). The C126 is the authority to write off the item of stores and legitimately order a replacement. The form also gives the Logistics Officer (LO) the authority to attribute an element of blame to the PLR custodian and recover a suitable amount of money from their pay. Accordingly, the custodian and, if necessary, their DO will have an opportunity to provide an explanation to try to reduce the recovery figure.

On this occasion the pipe has asked the Navigator to collect an item of stores. One navigator with whom I served lost his important slide rule down the back of his chart table and it was irretrievable. The slide rule slid because it is designed to slide, and was not secured for sea during a moment when the ship altered course across the sea and rolled. He, like the chefs (see page 62), was unhappy, but he, more than others, should have known better. Initially, I refused to write off the item of stores because the item was not technically lost, and could be recovered during the ship's next refit. I then had a word with myself, and I think the Captain had a word with me as well! I am not sure what accounting action we eventually took, but I am sure we did not fix the books (that never happened (ever)), and neither was the Navigator out of pocket. The slide rule may have been retrieved or, more likely, lost again when the ship was later scrapped. Maybe it will be dug up in several hundred years' time; the NATO stock number will help identify it.

Day 2

A Day Alongside is a Day Wasted

LOCATION: HIS MAJESTY'S NAVAL BASE DEVONPORT/AT SEA

'Special Sea Dutymen, close up, assume Damage Control State 3 Condition Yankee. Hands to Harbour Stations, hands to Harbour Stations. Hands out of the rig of the day, clear off the upper deck, close all screen doors and hatches.'

This pipe will also be annotated on Daily Orders as follows: 'SSDCUADCS3CYHTHSHTHSHOOTROTDCOTUDCASDAH'

This pipe means that the ship is about to go to sea or proceed alongside or undertake replenishment at sea; it is effectively a time when the ship is likely to be in confined waters or in very close proximity to other ships, and hence requires a greater number of personnel to be immediately available for seamanship activity and vital machinery availability.

The pipe is also directing certain members of the ship's company (Special Sea Dutymen, or SSDs) as directed by the Whole Ship Watch and Station Bill to proceed to their area of employment for such evolutions (for example, the Seamen/Warfare Ratings will proceed onto the upper deck to handle ropes, wires and anchor cables). The stokers will supervise engines and rudders. The WEs will monitor radio, sonar and radar serviceability. They will also provide a walkie talkie (which won't work). Logisticians will stay in bed. The aircrew, or Flight, will have disembarked at the earliest opportunity if homeward bounders, taking every conceivable piece of luggage with them.

Additionally, the pipe is directing that certain doors and hatches (those marked with a 'Y') be closed in order to heighten the ship's watertight integrity (Condition Yankee). Finally, it is directing those

A DAY ALONGSIDE IS A DAY WASTED

personnel who should not be on the upper deck (i.e. logisticians) to stay off the upper deck, and ensure all doors and hatches to the upper deck are shut.

For some, this pipe can be a sad moment – they might have just said 'goodbye' to their family before a long deployment. For others, having spent all of their ickies* and on the verge of bankruptcy after a particularly good run ashore, this will come as a relief. For the Caterer, going to sea means sadness as the catering account will start to experience actual 'expenditure'. The money in the catering account (while not real) seemingly belongs to the Caterer, and is guarded with zeal.

On completion of this serial (after the ship has docked/come to anchor/sailed into open water/finished replenishing), SSDs will fall out. This does not mean they have had an argument, but that they can now revert to cruising watches or look forward to a period of time ashore. Incidentally, if they do have an argument, it is likely that while 'Hands to Punching Stations' has not actually been piped, a fracas might have ensued. If both a Guzz and Pompey† ship are alongside in Gibraltar at the same time, some form of 'falling out' will have undoubtedly taken place. This might lead to another opportunity for the culprits to acquaint themselves with the Watch and Station Bill, which is usually situated on the bulkhead next to the Regulating Office, as they await a conversation with the Joss‡, followed by a visit to the Captain's Table.

'Smoke alarm, smoke alarm, smoke alarm, smoke alarm in the After Engine Room, location marking 4 Juliet.'

Having proceeded to sea, it is not unusual for the use of equipment such as engines to cause a fire. On this occasion, if at night, the pipe will have woken up most members of the ship's company and it will

---

* Foreign currency.
† Nickname for HMNB Portsmouth.
‡ Master at Arms.

instantly be accompanied by the ship's vent (air conditioning) being crash-stopped in order to prevent the spread of smoke. The pipe is informing the ship's company that smoke has been detected in the After Engine Room (AER), and the location of the compartment (4 Deck, Juliet Section) will direct personnel if they are unaware of the location of the AER.

This pipe might be followed by the General Alarm and the pipe: **'Fire, fire, fire, fire in the After Engine Room, location marking 4 Juliet. Attack Party muster at the scene, Support Party muster at the for'd section base. Containment Party muster in the weapon section base.'**

This pipe is telling the ship's company that there is a confirmed fire in the AER. It is directing certain members (as allocated by the Watch and Station Bill) to undertake certain actions. The Attack Party are the first responders; the Support Party take over from the Attack Party, and have been told to proceed to the forward (pronounced 'forad') section base where they will dress in enhanced protective equipment and breathing apparatus.

If the fire is located in the after end of the ship (the rear), the Support Party will dress in the forward section base (at the other end of the ship), and vice versa. The Containment Party's role is to monitor compartments on each side of the compartment in which the fire is located in order to monitor and prevent the spread of the fire: most compartments on a ship will have something dangerous on the other side of the bulkhead, such as the sea, a weapon magazine, a fuel tank or the Joss(!).

The fire is likely to be initially brought to the attention of the ship's company due to a loud vocal alarm – this is otherwise known as 'shouting'.

This is an unwelcome and worrying pipe. It is informing the ship that not only does it have a fire to contend with but it is likely to be a big fire, fuelled by oil. If this fire is not extinguished in minutes the ship is likely to be brought to Emergency Stations* due to its scale and impact.

---

* Ensuring that every member of the ship's company is ready for a large-scale firefighting effort. Not to be confused with Action Stations.

The Attack Party has 4.5 seconds (well, 2 minutes!) to make it to the scene of the incident, having taken care not to run. Personnel are always told not to run in order to prevent tripping etc. I suspect many do run – I walked fast (ran). The Support Party will have concurrently attempted to get changed into a Fearnought suit similar to that worn by Bungle from *Rainbow*. It will have been made from four million (well, several) compressed layers of wool. Incidentally, on one occasion a chief stoker (generally considered to be a firefighting deep specialist) briefed his firefighting team and said, 'This is a Fearnought suit, it will protect you from fire – it is made of compressed wool. Has anyone ever seen a sheep on fire? No? Good, let's go.'

Having also donned antiflash clothing and breathing apparatus, a chef will guess each firefighter's name and scribble their 'on air time' onto a board using a crayon (apparently somebody received a Herbert Lott award for inventing the special board, which uses some basic arithmetic and a dial to work out when the firefighting team will start to run out of air, and therefore when the next firefighting team needs to commence its journey to take over. This is aimed at ensuring a continuous aggressive attack on the fire in order to ensure that it has no chance of spreading). The Support Party has 8 seconds (well, 8 minutes) to do this while the ship is rocking from side to side.

If undertaking OST, and therefore not a real fire, it is likely that the searider* will have adjudged that the team has been 'beaten back' from the lit compartment. This requires a full re-entry to the compartment, which might take several hours and several re-entry teams, including officers *in extremis*. Helpfully, chefs will provide an urn of squash (aka water) to hydrate the firefighters.

As a Damage Control Officer (DCO) I would often go to bed with my overalls draped on a chair next to my bed so that in the event of a fire or flood, I could quickly slip into the overalls and head to HQ1 where my old pals Charge Chief Simpson and Buck Taylor and I would coordinate the damage control effort. On one such occasion, with an engine module fire at 0230, having accidentally placed my

---

* The independent instructor/assessor.

foot into a sleeve of my overalls instead of the leg, and unable to remove it, I hopped to HQ1 wearing a pair of Homer Simpson boxer shorts and my overalls being dragged behind me. Fortunately, as we waited for the engine space temperature to fall so that a re-entry could be made, I was greeted by Leading Chef Jan Donaldson who came to collect the Galley keys to make breakfast. He looked at me and asked: 'What are you doing dressed like that boss?'

Me: 'Coordinating damage control, Jan. Please ask one of the stewards to provide me with some clothing.'

Harbour FIREXs at OST are challenging. Typically, anybody who is not on duty will hastily leave the ship before the seariders turn up. They will return once the exercise is completed and will moan at the duty part (those on duty for 24 hours), who will probably have failed the exercise and have been 'rescrubbed', namely required to recomplete the exercise the following day. Cheers, Oppo!

'D'you hear there, DCO/OOD speaking. The fire is now out.'
This is an unsatisfactory pipe as, apparently, nobody actually understands what is meant by 'the fire is now out'. Indeed, far from easing troubled minds that a compartment is no longer ablaze, the good people at Flag Officer Sea Training (FOST) once stated that this phrase actually suggests to a Thesaurus-armed ship's company that the fire has escaped (i.e. it is out!) from the lit compartment and is now winding its merry way along 2 Deck, causing carnage to the highly polished flats which will then by ruined by fully charged hoses being dragged along them. This will disappoint the XO. If the flat is on 2 Deck the Warfare Officers will not be sad, as they do not know that such a deck exists.

Of course, the DCO or the OOD should have said that the fire has been 'extinguished'. That makes more sense. Therefore, if one hears the above pipe on a ship it is highly likely that it will be followed by:
'D'you hear there, DCO/OOD speaking. Amendment to the last pipe. The fire has been extinguished.'

A DAY ALONGSIDE IS A DAY WASTED

Very few people enjoy interacting with members of FOST who can be occasionally (very often) very pedantic. PO Steward Monty Mountford was once shouted at for producing a cabin cleaning card which stated that 'all cabins should be hoovered daily'. He was advised that the word 'hoovered' should be replaced by 'vacuumed' for fear of upsetting any other brand of vacuum cleaner. We sighed at this point and uttered words which require a different book to translate.

'D'you hear there, stand by for time check, in 10 minutes the time will be 0900Z …'
9 minutes pass.
'1 minute'
50 seconds pass.
'10 seconds'
5 seconds pass.
'5, 4, 3, 2, 1 Mark, the time is now 0900Z …'
'Good morning, this is the PWO in the Ops Room. Standby for SOCs Day 1, the area risk is red, EMCON plan 'apple' is in force – this is the least restricted plan.'
This Pipe is informing the ship's company that System Operator Checks (SOCs) are about to take place. Different SOCs take place on different days (e.g. Day 1, 2 etc.). The area risk state refers to threats from the enemy, and the EMCON plan refers to the emission control status of the ship (e.g. whether radars are transmitting). There are a number of aspects to this pipe.

Firstly, the time check itself will usually be made by a young sailor. It is normally conveyed in an articulate manner in the full knowledge that the main broadcast contains an amplification mode whereby people do not need to shout.

Secondly, to my knowledge nobody has ever synchronized their watches at this time.

Thirdly, the apparent upbeat 'good morning', and the rest of the pipe is given by the Principal Warfare Officer (PWO) who, for some reason, ignores the amplification equipment, and shouts.

It is also highly likely that one listener to the pipe will exclaim, 'Well of course the PWO is in the Ops Room ... where would you expect them to be, the Galley?'

The Operations Room, or Ops Room, is the compartment from where the ship fights its external battle. Within it will be employed Sonar, Radar, Weapon and Electronic Warfare Ratings. Depending on the particular type of ship, it might particularly specialize in a certain element of Warfare: for example, a destroyer will specialize in Above Water Warfare whereas a frigate is more likely to specialize in Under Water Warfare.

System Operator Checks (SOCs) involve checking whether everything that spins around, makes a noise or goes bang actually works. SOCs tends to involve a dawning realization that most of the equipment is broken. The list of defects is often considerable. The Weapon Engineering Officer (WEO) cries and then goes to sleep until the next set of SOCs.

SOCs commence with a test of the ship's general and chemical alarms. These alarms are tested on a routine basis to the extent that they can become a bit wearing. When they happen for real, other than when piped to Action Stations, the general alarm tends to come without warning. It is unpleasant and, literally, alarming. Typically, in HMS *Chatham*, the Marine Engineering Officer (MEO) appeared to train his engines to catch fire at lunchtime, just as I would have a post-lunch snooze!

At the end of SOCs, the PWO provides a list of defects to the Captain, who then tells people to fix the defects. The Jack Dusties raise requests for replacement stores at that point ... whether they are available is anyone's guess.

'Darken ship, darken ship. The whole of the upper deck is now out of bounds. Anybody wishing to proceed onto the upper deck must do so by first contacting the Officer of the Watch.'

This means that it is night time at sea and that personnel are not allowed on the upper deck.

The navigation lights will have been switched on and most of the WEs and Jack Dusties will have been 'in it' (in bed) for a fair few hours already. The Ship's Flight personnel (WAFUs)[*] will also be sleeping, and have been for most of the day. Despite the fire resistance of the old No. 4 (or No. 8) uniform, the ship's company junior rates will be wearing their 'Montrose Enterprises' (amend depending on the name of the particular ship) non-fire resistant t-shirts as they stroll about the ship. The members of the Wardroom will be wearing their Red Sea Rig[†], and it is highly likely that in the senior rates' mess they might not be wearing anything at all while listening to Neil Diamond or Glen Campbell. The highlight of an evening at sea might be the XO's evening pipe where they will have told the ship's company what happened today, and what is going to happen tomorrow. They will probably also have remarked that, 'Rounds were generally satisfactory this evening, but greater attention needs to be given in the corners of flats and passageways.'

In the passageways, the lighting changes from white lights to red lights.

Occasionally the evening's entertainment might consist of the ship's company quiz over the Ship's Radio Entertainment (SRE). The rules for this are fairly simple. The Wardroom never wins, but the CPOs' mess does. Everybody else just makes up the numbers.

Unless one is a watchkeeper, which may involve undertaking the Hey Diddle Diddle[‡], the ship's company goes to bed until it is awoken

---

[*] Ship's Flight personnel. The origins of the term 'WAFU' are unclear. Some believe it stands for 'Wet and Flaming Useless' although I was informed during my Naval History lessons at BRNC that the abbreviation originates from the evolving aviation activity onboard RN aircraft carriers during the interwar years. It was observed that the pioneering aviators would recover onboard (i.e. land) and the pilot would jump out demand more fuel and weapons so that he could get airborne and get back to the fight; hence Weapons and Fuel Users (WAFU).

[†] Reduced Sea Rig (nothing to do with the Red Sea) – black trousers, white short-sleeved shirt and ship's crested cummerbund.

[‡] Middle Watch. Often sailors will use a rhyming slang to refer to something e.g. 'The Middle [Watch]' is referred to as the 'Hey Diddle Diddle', even if it is actually longer that saying 'The Middle'!

by 'Call the Hands', a fire, flood or ship roll: whichever comes first. The Captain will be awoken by several shipping reports throughout the night, and at an additional time directed by the Captain (usually after 0700). For example, the Captain will have been awoken to be told that the sun has risen in the east and that the cloud coverage is 9/10ths. I was never quite sure why cloud coverage was such an immediate information requirement for the Captain.

Meanwhile, on the Bridge, the OOW, QM and BM will drink tea, spin dits (i.e. tell stories) and take a navigation fix. In the SCC, the stokers will be drinking tea and perhaps will dip a few tanks. For added joy, some members of the ship's company might be stripping and polishing a flat ready for a FIREX to take place the following day, during which hoses will be dragged across the deck, thereby undoing all of the good work.

Day 3

FOST are Here to Help!

LOCATION: AT SEA

'D'you hear there, the Thursday War brief will take place in the junior rates' dining hall at 2000. All key personnel are to attend.'

On this occasion, the ship is undertaking OST under the eyes of FOST. It never really felt like training. For many it felt like continuous cleaning, for some it felt as if they might be sacked, for everyone it felt as if they might have to do it all over again. However, FOSTies (seariders) insisted that they were 'here to help'. To any FOSTy reading this … you should have tried harder to land this message!

This pipe is summoning key members of the ship's company to be briefed on the weekly Thursday War which starts very early the following morning. The brief will start when the Captain arrives. The gathered personnel will be called to attention and many will not know whether to stand up or fold their arms. Some might do both.

The FOST syllabus itself contains every scenario that a ship may possibly face on a forthcoming deployment, ranging from basic safety at sea, cleaning, crowd control, food hygiene, noise hygiene, replenishing, damage control, counting things, warfighting, cleaning (again), meeting mayors, securing for action and cleaning.

OST is hard. It involves long days, long nights, and trying to be nice to people wearing berets and overalls (i.e. the seariders). The FOSTies usually arrive by boat. You can see them coming. You hope that the boat breaks. I used to try to muster a cheery 'good morning' to the staff, but I genuinely just wanted them to leave immediately – even the ones I knew and liked.

The Thursday War would take place on a ... Thursday. Sometimes there might be a Tuesday War as well. After one hour's sleep to get the ship looking like a new pin for a day of having charged hoses dragged along the decks, 'Call the Hands' will come all too soon. The ship's company will wear action coveralls (white for officers and warrant officers; blue for senior and junior ratings), antiflash protective clothing and a lifejacket, and will then proceed to their action station. This will typically be one of the following areas: the Bridge, the Operations Room, the weapon section base, various weapon or sensor compartments, Fire and Repair Party posts, machinery spaces, upper deck weapons, hangar. Depending on whether the ship is training to be in a chemical environment, personnel may carry a respirator as well. Some will also carry a hammer and wooden wedges. I used to carry pens and a rag and a laminated plan of the ship.

Most people will know their action station, although newcomers might need to acquaint themselves with the Watch and Station Bill. This document, usually attached to a bulkhead outside the Joss's office, will tell each person where they need to be for the various evolutions undertaken by the ship.

The ship will assume Chemical, Biological, Radiation, Nuclear, Damage Control (CBRNDC) State 1 Condition Zulu.[*] This means that everyone needs to be turned to, and all hatches and doors with a Z label (which is a marking attached to a watertight door and hatch) need to be shut with all clips tightened. These doors and hatches are shut in order to ensure that the ship can maximize its watertight integrity or indeed minimize the spread of smoke in case it is hit by a missile. Some doors and hatches, if containing the spread of smoke or part of a smoke clearance plan, will need a smoke sentry placed on them; this is a sailor whose express task is to make sure that no-one, under any circumstance, opens the door. Occasionally, some people will ignore the smoke sentry and breach the smoke clearance zone having just flown around the ship in a helicopter for a couple of hours (reducing a 'Good' serial to a 'Just satisfactory' serial).

During the Thursday War, the ship will fight an external battle, involving threats from above the sea (aircraft, missiles or drones), from on the sea (other ships or fast attack craft) and from below the surface of the water (submarines and mines). It will also fight an internal battle, involving concurrent fires, floods and casualties. The Caterer will use this as an opportunity to provide out-of-date action snacks ('nutty') to the ship's company.

Those not employed in the Operations Room will occasionally get a glimpse of how calm (or otherwise) things might be in the conduct of external battle when, during the PWO's update pipe, one might pick up in the background the shrill sound of the Electronic Warfare Rating's whistle followed by a vocal identification of an imminent threat, or they may hear the shout 'ORS!' (i.e. the PWO is trying to speak to Operations Room Supervisor, who is responsible for co-ordinating the multiple enemy action and weapon updates).

Amid the humour and reflections of days gone by in the Navy, which I hope emerge from these pipe recollections, my other memory of OST is that I often thought that I could indeed be doing this for real one day. I am fairly certain that most of my matelot friends will

---

[*] 'State' is referring to the personnel readiness of the ship.

have gone to Action Stations for real (or 'safeguard') during their careers, and the General Alarm will still spark their senses.

At the end of the Thursday War, the key members of the ship's company will gather in a compartment to hear the feedback from the FOSTies. The Captain will politely thank them for their efforts, although in reality the Captain will want rid of them as well. They will then board their boat armed with their bag meals so that they can go back to FOST HQ and write or cut and paste their reports.

A FOST debrief is an uneasy moment, and will cause many a murmur and scowl. On one particular occasion, during which HMS *Somerset* had successfully shot down everything that the enemy could muster, and had fought every fire and flood without anyone breaching smoke boundaries (WAFUs, note please), the CO was particularly saddened to note the following assessment from the Warrant Officer Caterer: '… you may have won the external and internal battle today, Sir, but for me the war was lost as soon as I came onboard and found a baked bean in the dishwasher filter.'[*]

Prior to OST, the FOST staff might issue a handy 'Common Pick-Ups' list that enables ships and submarines to identify issues which can be easily addressed and make their lives easier. One typical pick-up from daily assessments is that '… the ship's company lacked a sense of urgency'.

As a result, the good ship HMS *Argyll* once created Sense of Urgency parties to rush about and look busy.

I myself was saddened when the FOST Team advised that when delivering positive news, such as a fire being extinguished (not 'out'!), I should stop saying, 'This is DCO with good news …'

Apparently this was not the done thing.

Eventually, OST would end and the Admiral (Flag Officer Sea Training) would gather the ship's company on the flight deck to tell them that they were 'Just satisfactory' because, despite amassing a string of 'Good' assessments, they once received a solitary 'Just sat' for leaving a towel unattended or a locker unlocked. Unless the ship has failed, many people will probably care little for this

---

[*] While this might appear to be a joke, it was not.

speech. Either the ship will proceed on deployment shortly after, or a Pompey ship will put on 'Pompey revs' (go fast) and go back to its base port.

Some non-matelots may wonder why FOSTies are not liked. In short, they have an extraordinary power to ruin weekends or indeed, if absolutely required, assess that a person should be removed from their assignment; such cases are rare, but in fairness, are occasionally necessary.

'The safeguard rule is now in force.'

During a period when a ship is undertaking exercises (such as OST), in the event of a real emergency or incident the pipe is prefixed 'Safeguard, safeguard, safeguard'. This means that there really is a fire, flood, casualty or similar, and rather than let the duty watch crack on and deal with the incident, there is a good chance that there will be a requirement for everybody to take part, including the officers and perhaps even the EWO.

Therefore, at the end of the Thursday War brief, or very shortly after 'Call the Hands' on the Thursday, the 'Safeguard' pipe will be made, and once the war is at an end the following will be piped: **'The safeguard rule is no longer in force.'**

'Kings to Action Messing.'

During times of heightened tension (i.e. a risk of engaging with the enemy) a ship might fall into Defence Watches (when half of the ship's company is on watch while the others sleep), and sometimes Action Stations (when the whole of the ship's company is on watch, dispersed around the ship ready to fight the enemy or deal with fires or floods). Action Stations, and the ability to defeat an enemy at sea, is the key element of OST.

While I have given FOSTies deserved grief during this series of pipes, I have always felt that their provision of Action Stations training provided an eerie sense of realism, and having mercifully only been to Action Stations for real on three occasions, I felt as prepared as I could be.

Time at Action Stations can be lengthy, tiring or indeed boring.

I have always admired how articulate the PWO was when piping 'Action Stations'. It would typically go as follows: **'D'you hear there, intelligence suggests that the enemy is building a raid from the east, and it is likely that the ship will come under attack, THEREFORE, hands to Action Stations, hands to Action Stations!'**

It was the 'therefore' bit that always tickled me. No variation at all. The PWO could have used 'thus' or 'consequently', but in any event I am glad that the order was linked to the operational context by the word 'therefore'. It gave it all meaning. Neville Chamberlain did the same but used 'consequently' when he was in the Cabinet Room of 10 Downing Street.

Amid all of the ensuing action or inaction comes the requirement to eat. Action Messing takes RN catering to an entirely different height or depth.

During a 'lull' in the action the PWO, having consulted (or not) the LO, will pipe 'Action Messing'. Until that point the Galley will have been secured (vacated, with all equipment shut down). At this point the Galley is opened, but only the most basic of ingredients and equipment are used, so that it can be closed away with the minimum of fuss or hazard should enemy activity dictate at short notice. As a result, the food, while nutritious, is typically some form of hotpot or pasta dish accompanied by a piece of ripe or overripe fruit.

In order to strike an appropriate balance between ensuring suitable coverage in key positions of the ship and allowing for people to be fed, only a quarter of the ship's company are allowed to eat at any one time. A number of different techniques are used to ensure this balance is met, ranging from the allocation of playing cards to pure guesswork. Thus (or 'therefore'), the pipe 'Kings [or Queens/Clubs/Spades] to Action Messing' which means that only those personnel possessing the appropriate card will be spared to go and eat. Occasionally an unscrupulous sailor might have obtained a card of each suit.

Having arrived at the dining hall, the diners will be shouted at by the Joss or EWO. They will be required to take a paper plate and plastic fork. The fork is likely to break during the meal. They will be provided with a hot meal usually cooked to the surface temperature of the sun. As they will be given a very short amount of time (i.e. a few minutes) to eat, it is likely that third degree burns will be sustained in the process of ingestion. People are not allowed to converse during this time: just eat.

Helpfully, the FOSTies will determine whether the food has been cooked to the correct temperature and will ensure that the chefs probe the food (although I am not certain that chefs would have the time to probe food if the ship is actually under attack).

It is during these moments that shipmates from other parts of the ship will briefly come together wearing their antiflash clothing. People will usually exchange a knowing glance and if undertaking training, as opposed to the real thing, they might enquire, 'How's it been going, shippers?'; the answer is usually, 'Shit, mate!' One lucky sailor may be designated as a casualty, and having been applied with make-up to simulate an injury, will have spent the day sleeping in a compartment.

An LO's reputation and subsequent promotion opportunities can be defined by a single serial of Action Messing. So, to the chefs of HMS *Chatham*, I owe it all to you (and the Jack Dusties, Writers and stewards before you all grumble). In fact I think Jack Dusties did a stint in the Galley at Action Messing – I can name two who I would not really want to be involved in any form of cookery (and a few chefs for that matter).

'Action Snacks, Action Snacks!'

This is one of the oddest pipes heard onboard, and indeed not every ship will pipe 'Action Snacks', but instead will let sailors determine when is an appropriate time to eat a bar of chocolate that they have been provided with to tide them over until the provision of a more substantial meal.

In times of conflict, and at Action Stations as detailed in a previous pipe (page 50), a ship's sailors will be dispersed throughout the ship ready to fight enemies, fires and floods. For some, this can be a lonely time, and, for all, a frightening time.

Action Snacks is aimed at providing much needed sustenance until a substantial meal can be prepared (through Action Messing), and a morale boost. At a certain time in the action (usually when the Captain becomes hungry), the command decision is made for people to eat their bar of chocolate. While several varieties of chocolate exist, Action Snacks are usually Mars, Snickers, Yorkie or Picnic. Typically the chocolate is out of date, and sometimes it is inedible.

Action Snacks are a cause of great consternation and, like Action Messing, can make or break a LO's time onboard; the issue of a 'Fudge' bar was once poorly received, and the existence of a Flake in the Operations Room also caused upset. Should the CO ever order 'Action Snacks' twice during the Thursday it will almost certainly move the PO Caterer to tears. Some LOs wisely insist on 'touch drills' only (i.e. let's not eat the chocolate for real!).

'Casualty, casualty, casualty, casualty in One Mike Flat.'
This means that somebody has hurt themselves on 1 Deck, Mike Section. Every emergency incident, whether it is a fire, flood or casualty, is piped by stating what the incident is and its location. The flat is not an apartment, but a nice shiny deck which is polished often (which has probably led to the casualty slipping and causing the injury).

There are lots of flats in a ship.

The tiller flat is where the steering can be controlled in emergency (at some effort I might add). This is one of the loneliest places to be placed at Action Stations, and tends to be given to Clubz[*].

The canteen flat contains the NAAFI or 'the Colonel', which refers to the former dictator Colonel Gaddafi (which rhymes with NAAFI). Very similar to Colonel Gadaffi, the CANMAN (i.e. the canteen manager) also has a dictatorial approach to life, and opens and closes when they wish as opposed to the opening times displayed on the bulkhead outside of the NAAFI. This is a bit like the Ship's Office. The Colonel is a valuable addition to the ship: it provides

---

[*] The Physical Training Instructor because of their 'guns'!

discounted cigarettes, possibly slush puppies, lighters, pot noodles, beer, goffas and nutty. In Guzz, Ivor Dewdney pasties would also be provided as welcome sustenance after the previous night in Jesters (a popular nightclub on Union Strip in Devonport).

The Wardroom flat is in officer country. Only officers and dutymen are allowed in this area of the ship.

Back to the casualty ...

The ship has its own rudimentary ambulance service and upon hearing the casualty pipe, the ship's Petty Officer Medical Assistant (POMA) or Leading Medical Assistant (LMA), chefs and stewards rush to the scene in order to provide first aid. At this time if a medical doctor (MO) is embarked, they will reach the scene of the incident once their game of uckers[*] has been completed.

The reader will now be aware that as well as performing their primary roles, many sailors undertake key secondary roles onboard requiring significant extra training. They do, however, get paid the same as their Army and RAF counterparts who do not have such extra responsibilities.

Some years ago I escorted an Army brigadier to a warship. During the visit, he witnessed Action Stations and noted that one of the ship's stewards was also first aid responder. He also noted that the well-built Fijian sailor was probably a rugby player. He then asked the sailor why he did not join the Army instead of the Navy (presumably on the basis that the Army's focus was predominantly on winning the Army v Navy match).

The sailor replied, 'Because I think the Army is a bit shit if I'm honest, Sir.' Sailors are usually fairly honest folk. I laughed. The brigadier did not.

(To note. We do like the Army and we tend to take pity on them when they live in holes, and sometimes we like the Crabs[†] especially when they fly us home – usually late).

---

[*] Uckers is a board game based on Ludo played throughout the Fleet.
[†] The RN refers to the RAF as 'Crabs'.

Day 45

Hold On (Literally), the Heads are Out of Action

LOCATION: AT SEA

'RAS Special Sea Dutymen close up, assume Damage Control State 3, Condition Yankee.'

This pipe is similar to an earlier pipe (page 40), and is informing the ship's company that certain personnel are required in positions to enable the ship to replenish (i.e. refuel and or provision) while at sea. It may be followed a little later, and at various intervals by: **'D'you hear there, no smoking, no naked lights throughout the ship, refuelling ship.'**

Running out of fuel on a ship can be challenging. Firstly, unless one relies on the tidal flow, the ship needs power to move and fight. Secondly, if the ship does not have any fuel, it is likely to enter a state of loll and capsize.

The ship can obtain fuel at extortionate rates from the nearest port or can replenish at sea with the helpful support of the Royal Fleet Auxiliary (RFA). RFA people are like RN sailors except they have windows/scuttles in their cabins, ensuite bathrooms, fresh fruit and flexible tax arrangements. Some also used to have porn-star moustaches.

Replenishing at sea is known as RASing. When a ship conducts a RAS it passes fuel or stores (and occasionally people!) via ropes and wires between the ships. It is dangerous and testing.

The risks of RASing are multiple, ranging from death by falling over the side, collision, fire, boredom, hyperthermia or hypothermia or sunstroke. On this occasion, the warning pipe is directing people not to smoke or have naked lights on the upper deck in order to prevent the ignition of fuel fumes (see Ghost Pipes, from page 124).

HOLD ON (LITERALLY), THE HEADS ARE OUT OF ACTION

The opportunities on the other hand are also appealing, ranging from a suntan, ice cream, fuel, stores, food and toilet rolls.

During an RAS, a sailor will shoot a projectile (which unfortunately resembles a phallus) from a rifle from the warship to the RFA ship. The projectile carries a line which in turn is connected to other lines which have different purposes, such as a phone line, a distance measuring line and a line over which stores can be passed. After a number of attempts, taking cover and whistles being blown, lines will eventually be passed and fuel will be topped up. There are key people in this evolution: the dabbers (who actually know what is happening); the XO or LO (who is the safety officer and doesn't really know what is happening); the Captain (who drives the ship); the Leading Steward (who holds a board containing the course and speed of the ship, and provides tea); the Bunting Tosser (the member of the Communications Branch who hoists and lowers Flag Romeo (i.e. a particular flag used to co-ordinate movements of the ships)); everyone else (who tend ropes and wires, maybe steal choc ices, steer the ship and count stores).

The members of each ship's company can wave at other human beings (who probably won't wave back), and the captains can exchange a bottle of whisky which they generally share widely.[*]

Depending on what items are being transferred, the RAS can take several hours, and once it has been completed, the ships will part company at which point the following will be piped: **'RAS Special Sea Dutymen fall out. Revert to Damage Control State 3, Condition X-Ray.'**

'D'you hear there, Captain speaking ...'

These words alone are enough to stop sailors in their tracks or wake Jack Dusties up from their sleep in the Clothing Store.

There are two extraordinary issues with this pipe. Firstly, the frequency of a Captain making a pipe is similar to that of a solar

---

[*] Rarely (if ever).

eclipse. Secondly, it rarely heralds good news. For land lubbers, it is like a newsflash during *Coronation Street*.

If the Captain's pipe is to convey bad news, it is likely to mean that we are at war, someone has died, or, worse, the ship's programme has changed. The pipe will have probably been preceded by 'galley buzzes' (rumours). It might also be preceded by the pipe: **'The Operations Officer is requested to report to the Captain's cabin.'**

It will then be followed by the pipe: **'All heads of department are requested to report to the Captain's cabin.'**

This means that the MEO will need to get changed out of smelly overalls, the LO will need to stop counting stuff and the WEO will require a shake (i.e. be woken up). The Flight Commander will stir from their deckchair or halt the game of uckers with the MO. It will be for the Operations Officer ('Ops') to try to make a start on how to reconfigure the ship's programme.

Like the ship's weekly menu, the ship's programme is subject to change at short notice. Typically, a change to a programme involving a wholesale change to a planned deployment will involve no longer going to a fun place (such as the West Indies, or global deployment), and will be replaced by ... the Gulf or the Falklands. It might also mean that if one is in a Guzz ship, the deployment to the West Indies is now being undertaken by a Portsmouth-based ship, which adds insult to injury!

Going to the Gulf is challenging. It is quite dangerous, very hot, very expensive and, at times, when on patrol, fairly mundane. For those who enjoy alcohol, such indulgence comes at a premium. It may not even happen at all.

Occasionally the Captain might take an even greater step and meet the ship's company in the flesh at a 'clear lower deck' on the flight deck or in the hangar to speak to them in person. During such gatherings, the ship's company will muster in groups according to their rank or rate. Having arrived and stepped onto a raised platform like Jesus on the Mount, the Captain will usually tell the ship's company to break ranks and come closer. At this point some comedians will make sheep noises. A sweepstake might have taken place on what news the Captain will impart.

Among other things, a sea freight container containing toilet rolls, destined for a planned rendezvous in a port, might now never find its way to the ship.

After this pipe, it is likely that the ship will alter course ...

'D'you hear there, the ship is about to alter course across the sea, and may roll heavily.'

This pipe is intended to be a helpful warning from the OOW that the ship is about to alter course, during which it may move beam-on (sideways) to the sea. This is an uncomfortable moment.

The OOW's use of the word 'may' should invariably be replaced by the word 'will' or indeed 'has just rolled'.

Violent movements caused by the sea can cause injury. Indeed if, for example, one has not secured a towel, the towel could cause serious injury (though I was never sure how!) or clog up a water extraction pump. *In extremis* (i.e. war), a ship will secure for action, meaning everything that is likely to move will be lashed to the deck or bulkhead or removed from sight.

The alteration of course usually takes place while the chefs are preparing lunch, and if one is fortunate enough to be stood outside the Galley at the time of this pipe, or shortly after, it is likely that one will hear colourful language alongside the clatter of pans hitting the deck. The expletives are likely to be of greater severity and volume if the warning pipe is made after the alteration of course. Fortunately, if the food has been delayed or spoiled it is likely to be viewed sympathetically by the rest of the ship's company who will have patiently queued for lunch from 1100.

Seasickness can be brought on by the ship rolling. It typically has three stages:

1. Being physically sick.
2. A mortal fear of dying.
3. A mortal fear of not dying.

Life goes on during times of heavy sea states and although, for some, particularly WEs, WAFUs and logisticians, their duties should enable them to sleep through the inclement conditions; others might find themselves on the Bridge with a bucket beside them.

HOLD ON (LITERALLY), THE HEADS ARE OUT OF ACTION

It is not unknown for the PO Caterer to use a period of rough weather to put kippers on for breakfast.

'D'you hear there, the for'd heads will be out of action until further notice.'

This is a disappointing pipe especially if the ship has just rolled heavily. It means that the heads in the forward section of the ship are not working. They are either undergoing planned maintenance or have been blocked by someone flushing a paper towel (rather than toilet paper) down the toilet. Mercifully, I have never had to perform the role of unblocking the foreign body. I have, though, had to clean heads and bathrooms for 12 weeks as a cadet, and was appointed as Captain Heads and Bathrooms (which was not actually a joke!).

My guess is that this task is very unpleasant and only mitigated by the fact that the maintainers will be able to claim 'pay for work of an unpleasant nature' at £1.04 per day. In order to claim this pay, it will be necessary to raise a form and have it signed by least three people (one of whom must hold the rank of captain). This will provide excessive work for the PO or CPO Writer (almost certainly into the Dogs), but will also enable the maintainers of the heads and bathrooms to have more ickies for the next run ashore.

The temporary closure of the heads will be a challenge for some. It will mean that some will either wish to 'hold on', or *in extremis*, venture to the aft end of the ship to the other set of heads. Those officers not used to going onto 2 Deck (i.e. Warfare Officers) might need help locating the heads if they are aft of the Colonel.

The heads are relatively austere. They have a very powerful suction system which, I am told, should not be used while sitting on the toilet itself. Helpfully, the inside door of the cubicle (or 'trap') will contain reading material ranging from *Rules of the Road* to *Flight Safety*. If one is using the heads and the air conditioning suddenly stops, and that person is part of the Standing Sea Emergency Party (the SSEP), this might prove exceptionally challenging in meeting the Standard Fleet Time. The SSEP are at immediate notice to deal with most emergencies onboard while at sea, and they are required to arrive at the incident in a short period of time (known as the Standard Fleet Time). Invariably, if the air conditioning suddenly stops (known as a crash stop) without warning, it indicates that a fire has occurred, as the crash stop aims to prevent the spread of smoke. Hence, being caught short in the heads will be a challenge for the SSEP. Other sailors are likely to laugh at their oppo's plight rather than necessarily worry about the fire or flood.

Within the compartment might also be found the showers. The showers will have a privacy curtain and a mat with a plastic cable tie attached which enables it to be hung on the bulkhead to dry. If there is a row of showers, and it is Harry Roughers (rough sea) in older ships, as well as having the water from one's own shower swish around one's feet one may have the gentle wave of the adjacent showers pass forward to aft, and vice versa, during the shower. There is an occasional call of 'yellow river' which is why the use of shower 'bats' (footwear) is advised. As one commences/finishes the shower one should shout 'switching on'/'switching off' to alert an adjacent user to the potential for a change in pressure or heat. I still occasionally consider doing this at home, but no longer wear flip flops. Neither do I have to climb through a kidney hatch wearing only a towel to get to the ablutions.

During Captain's Rounds*, the heads are spotless. During one such serial, having taped off the heads to prevent usage before the Captain inspected them, I found the Bish[†] to be in one of the traps despite the yellow 'DO NOT USE' tape on the door. To this day, I have no idea how he got there. An act of God perhaps.

The pipe **'The for'd heads are back in bounds'** will come as a relief to everyone. Later in the evening the First Lieutenant is likely to mention this in their evening pipe, and will remind people that only toilet paper is to be deposited down the heads. They will repeat the pipe many times during the deployment.

The likely reason for the blockage to the ship's heads is a foreign object being disposed of into the ship's sewage treatment system.

---

* The Captain's formal inspection of the ship.
† The Chaplain.

HOLD ON (LITERALLY), THE HEADS ARE OUT OF ACTION

There are a number of possible causes. Occasionally, people will place kitchen/paper hand towels into the toilet rather than toilet roll. I am unsure why one would choose to use kitchen roll (unless there is a shortage of actual toilet roll; see page 87), not least because the material is rough and coarse.* Other items might fall from one's pocket and into the heads; for example, a comb or a mobile telephone. From time to time a sailor might take an item from the 'special interest/top row' section of Daily Editorials (see page 31), and the magazine will usually be placed in the back of their trousers during the transit to the heads. People also have a habit of placing their beret at the back of their trousers. Both of these items are known to have blocked the ship's sewage system. It is not unusual for personnel to place items of underwear into the system. Fortunately, with correctly labelled kit (see page 74), it will be easy to determine the culprit.

There are various methods used to unblock the sewage treatment system but it typically relies on the use of a 'sani snake' or a hand pump with a rubber seal which blasts the toilet with low pressure air. Unfortunately, it does not matter whether the maintainer swings from the deck head or has the reflexes of a fly, as they invariably become covered in the contents of the system. It truly is work of an unpleasant nature and deserving of the extra £1.04 per day in the pay packet.

Occasionally, the pipe will be slightly amended by a witty sailor as follows: **'D'you hear there, the for'd heads will be out of action for the next 45 minutes, all users are requested to log off.'**

This pipe is intended to be a witty alternative to a pipe associated with planned maintenance of the ship's computer system, OASIS. When OASIS was due to be maintained, it would be necessary to warn users to save their work and log off in order to prevent losing their day's/life's work. However, on this occasion, the insertion of 'log off' has an entirely different meaning relating to one's bodily movements.

---

* Although a Pusser's toilet roll could hardly be described as quilted.

'D'you hear there, NAMET maths classes will take place in the junior rates' dining hall at 1600.'

This pipe is informing the ship's company that a period of maths instruction will be taking place at 1600. A witty sailor might add, 'that is when the big hand is on the 12 and the small hand is on the 4' and will subsequently be rebriefed.

Sailors join the RN with varying levels of qualifications. Some join with very little and leave with degrees. In addition to providing the opportunity to study and learn a range of subjects (many of which it will fund), the RN used to have its own Naval Maths and English Test (NAMET), and reaching a certain standard would determine one's eligibility for promotion. It was considered by some that those sailors with a poor NAMET score were not particularly bright, hence the additional emboldened text to the pipe was occasionally added to try to poke fun at the attendees to NAMET Maths.

Some periods at sea can be mundane, and on long passages between ports or on patrol a number of activities will be devised to fill the time productively, such as education lessons. Volunteers would be sought to provide tuition for personnel, and they would receive an allowance for it. Education Officers* might also be embarked (should the deployment be to somewhere sunny).

WARNING – this pipe is usually made in a very loud voice.

'D'you hear there, Clubz speaking, circuits will take place on the flight deck at 1700. All are welcome.'

This pipe has been made by the Clubswinger, aka Clubz (the ship's Physical Training Instructor). Clubz will have attended a course at HMS *Temeraire*, at which they will have learned to talk loudly, often in a manner which people cannot understand. They will also have

---

* Schoolies.

learned to salute with a funny leg movement and their hands placed on their feet or knees. In addition, they will have learned the Horn Pipe dance.

Clubz has four important roles in a ship. Firstly, producing Daily Orders (variously known as Daily Dits, Daily Words or Daily Lies); this is the ship's programme for the following day. Secondly, as the SSD QM, they will help drive the ship at Specials (moments when you need a light and skilled hand on the helm). The RN chooses not to use one of the Cruising Watch QMs for this delicate manoeuvre (despite the fact that it is effectively their day job). Thirdly, Clubz helps keep the ship's company fit by organizing circuits on the flight deck, and occasionally organizing flight deck sport (subject of another pipe, see page 77). They will also organize a fitness test, usually on the jetty of a dusty port in baking heat. Though times are a-changing, while the rest of the ship's company would wear No. 4s or 8s at sea (for their protective fire-retardant qualities), Clubz would typically wear a vest and shorts. Fourthly, Clubz is usually responsible for organizing the disposal of gash (see page 108).

Circuits typically takes place on the flight deck. Submarines do not have a flight deck or a Clubswinger. They keep fit by rowing in the Bomb Shop while personnel-under-training sleep underneath a torpedo.

Circuits is not compulsory, but the Royal Navy Fitness Test (RNFT) is. Attendance at Circuits varies. A hard core of four sailors will be there irrespective of the sea state, as will any Royal Marine who is embarked. Prior to their annual RNFT, others might attend in a state of panic. Additionally, towards the end of a deployment, attendance might increase as sailors attempt to remove evidence of runs ashore from their waistline. The CO may attend, and the other participants will marvel in wonder at the CO's PT rig.

Circuits involves a set of different exercises. Some will lift weights, some will attempt squat thrusts and others will run around the upper deck. This is a challenge, as the deck is often moving. Conducting a squat thrust at 45 degrees is particularly challenging, especially if the OOW has altered course across the sea. Running around the upper deck comes at great peril. Daily Orders should have informed the ship's company whether runners will run clockwise or anti-clockwise on a particular day. This will enable one to determine which door they should open onto the upper deck. Occasionally, Daily Words are careless cut and paste documents, and will mislead door openers, or door openers simply will not have read Daily Orders. Either scenario might lead to a heavy metal door being opened in the face of an oncoming runner. That will hurt.

The runner will run past a series of air outlets on the upper deck, some of which expel hot air, and some of which expel cool air. This can be a help or a hindrance depending on whether one is at sea in the Gulf or the Polar region. Some of the outlets will also expel the fragrance of 'evening scran' from the Galley.

The less fit personnel (i.e. 50 per cent of the ship's company) may attend 'Huffers and Puffers'. Huffers and Puffers is designed to be less rigorous. Unfortunately, this will often take place at lunchtime when most people not on watch are eating scran, at the NAAFI getting nutty or either 'in it' or 'on it'. Hence it will be poorly attended, which explains why the participants qualify for being at Huffers and Puffers in the first place.

Although it is not officially part of their duties, Clubz might also organize the ship's company quiz.

Day 46

What is a Flight Deck Actually for Anyway?

LOCATION: AT SEA

'Hands to flying stations, hands to flying stations. Gash is not to be ditched. No smoking on the upper desk abaft the funnel.'

This means that the ship is about to prepare to launch or recover its helicopter, and certain personnel are to undertake duties to support this. It also means that rubbish is not to be dropped into the sea (in order to prevent ingestion into aircraft engines), and that smoking is not to take place towards the aft end of the ship.

In reality the pipe means that the ship is about to receive its long-awaited mail. Many RN ships are cleverly designed to have their own mail collection service using a helicopter. Occasionally, typically on a monthly basis, the helicopter will also be launched to take part in an exercise in finding surface foes or, if it is really pushing the boundaries, a submarine. A Merlin helicopter is especially good at finding submarines (but it will need to have inflated its tyres after exiting the hangar (good design oversight!)).

The people who fly and maintain the ship's helicopter are called the Ship's Flight, and they are lucky. They are known as WAFUs. They visit the ship for a holiday, and they bring their deckchairs. They also have lots of sleep, get paid more money than everyone else and if they have less than 48 hours sleep in a 60-hour cycle they are allowed to go on strike. Going on strike is known as 'Aircraft on Ground' (AOG). It can last for several days, and technically means that the helicopter is broken. This usually means that the Jack Dusties have to find a spare part for the helicopter. Magically, if the ship comes close to land, especially the UK or somewhere

WHAT IS A FLIGHT DECK ACTUALLY FOR ANYWAY?

nice and warm, the aircraft will become sufficiently serviceable for it to undertake 'one Flight only', and will enable the WAFUs to get ashore or go home.

The Ship's Flight live in the hangar, a special part of the ship which has its own ecosystem, language and rules. The Ship's Flight can, for example, ignore other aspects of the ship's life, such as smoke boundaries during an important fire exercise.

The other clever people who form part of the Ship's Flight who watch the helicopter launch and recover, and who climb over the helicopter, are mechanics and engineers. The RN will typically assign four or five of these people to maintain the helicopter on a frigate or destroyer. The RAF will use double the number per aircraft. Nobody knows why there is such a disparity in numbers.

The Flight Deck Officer (FDO) is responsible for providing instructions to the pilot to enable them to successfully recover the aircraft. While the FDO provides these helpful instructions there is no guarantee of them being followed.

In order to prevent foreign objects being ingested into the helicopter's engines (which is known as Foreign Object Damage, i.e. FOD) some sailors search the upper deck of the ship to pick up FOD; this is known as FODPLOD. It is unknown whether schoolchildren or those in distress undertake FODPLOD when helicopters visit schools or storm-ravaged parts of the world.

'D'you hear there, a church service will take place in the senior rates' dining hall in 5 minutes' time. All are welcome.'

Within the day-to-day bustle of activity on a ship at sea on deployment, Church still takes place whether on passage or on operations. In reality, very few people tend to attend church services, either because they are not Christian or because they are on watch or in bed.

There are a number of almighty forces that influence the life of a sailor: the Captain, the Departmental Coordinator (DEPCO) and God if one is a Christian.

If a Bish is not embarked, a junior officer will be invited/told to provide a church service often irrespective of whether the officer holds any particular faith or belief.

Each week a mess will be invited to sponsor the service.[*] Such a commitment entails arranging and securing the tables and chairs, giving readings, making tea and, if it is the chiefs' mess sponsoring the service, wobbly coffees are often provided on completion. Attendance at the S&S mess-sponsored church services (logistics' mess in old money) is usually higher due to the provision of stickies (i.e. cake).

Any member of the ship's company with a very basic aptitude for playing an instrument will be a helpful addition to the throng. Alternatively, an ability to work a CD player is helpful. Sometimes the Bish might choose hymns that people actually know.

A Bish might come and go according to the ship's programme. Typically, one can expect to see the Bish embark in the Mediterranean during the summer, or in the Far East, but they won't necessarily be seen climbing the Gangway in Faslane before Ex Joint Warrior[†]. The same can be said of dentists, schoolies and other visitors, many of whom seem to choose their timing based on where the ship is in the world. Visitors are generally welcome onboard, apart from the SIB[‡], squadron officers, FOSTies, admirals and HMRC. Welcome guests might involve expats evacuated from areas of unrest, sea cadets or some of the guests from a cocktail party … although, to this day, it is unclear how five 'working ladies' found their way into the HMS *Somerset*'s cocktail party in Rio in 1999.

The RN is fortunate to have had many legendary chaplains. Some of them took their understanding of wine and bread especially seriously, particularly the former component, and there are many ratings and officers who have welcomed the padre's support or a boiled sweet as they have trudged across Dartmoor.

---

[*] Typically a ship has the following messdeck set up (or slight variations): Wardroom, warrant officers' and CPOs' mess, POs' mess, logistics' mess, stokers' mess, WEs' mess, girls' mess.
[†] An exercise off Scotland.
[‡] Special Investigation Branch (men in shiny suits).

Dartmoor, incidentally, is where the Navy sends its trainees to toughen up during initial training. It has little resemblance to the sea other than being cold and wet. However, on Dartmoor the officers in particular can learn the art or science of elementary bomb disposal by taking a bomb, suspending it over a hole and rotating it three times clockwise followed by four times anti-clockwise.

Many chaplains are fine men and women, with deep dedication and courage, and often great fun and genuine morale force multipliers. They are also very good at uckers!

On one occasion, in the Arabian Sea, a ship suffered a defect to its refrigeration and air conditioning system, leading to the ship becoming incredibly hot. During one church service at that time, the Bish stood in front of a hot and sweaty congregation in their tropical white uniforms. At that point he took out a can of Coca Cola and asked whether 'it' was the real thing, or whether God was the 'real thing'*. He then drank the can of Coca Cola. No one laughed, least of all the Captain.

'D'you hear there, laundry is now ready for collection.'
This somewhat innocuous pipe will mask a number of fears. Will my clothes, especially my civvies, be the same colour and size prior to their being submitted? Will all of the buttons still be in place? Will I be able to understand the scribble on the associated chit (telling me the cost)? If my dhobeying (laundry) has not come back on time, has my risk of submitting most of my underwear not paid off? Why is my white shirt now yellow? How do my black socks not get mixed up with other black socks? Why do my jeans have a crease on them (not that officers wear jeans/denim – read on …)? Why do my clothes smell like a bakery?

Dhobeying (cleaning) one's uniform is important. It ensures that one's uniform is clean and presentable, and does not degrade.

---

* The 'real thing' being Coke's campaign line in 2003.

That said, RN uniform often does not fit or meet its purpose from the outset! For example, some items of uniform have pockets on the thigh, inner leg, shin, and upper arm. Most of the pockets cannot be reached, and will never be used.

If one's uniform is not labelled, the Joss will be cross. Working uniform (e.g. No. 4s, 8s, ovvies (i.e. overalls), chefs' whites) should have one's name above the left-hand breast pocket. In days gone by, it would often be scrawled illegibly on a tatty white strip. The CO's name would have been perfectly written by a Tudor monk. WAFUs would have their wings stitched above their made-up name so that (in case it is not apparent by their swagger, pay and unfamiliarity with the ship other than the Wardroom or hangar), one can tell that they are pilot or observer. Many WAFUs have a made-up name which bears very little resemblance to their actual first name, for example: 'Damage' (based on features), 'Jive' (based on surname – Bunny), 'Bouncy' (based on surname – Castle), 'Pretty Boy' (based on features), 'Lemon' (based on surname – Curd), 'Beaky' (based on features), 'Wimpy' (based on surname – Holmes), 'Boogie' (based on surname – Knight).

A range of badges may be appended to a uniform to denote the achievement of a qualification, or one's branch, or good behaviour. Good Conduct Badges are awarded for every four years of good conduct up to and including 12 years. So, for 12 years+ service of good conduct a sailor (up to the rank of petty officer) will have three chevron badges. It may make them look like a sergeant in the Army and RAF, but in actual fact it means that they never got caught doing anything wrong, and were actually quite intelligent, which is why they joined the RN rather than the junior Services. After 15 years they may be granted the Long Service and Good Conduct Medal. This used to be awarded only to ratings, as it was assumed the officers' behaviour was always exemplary; this was a flawed assumption.

In the past other items of uniform were issued which did not technically meet the Trade Descriptions Act or were designed by the BeeGees, or Victorians, or were only for men: foulies (i.e foul weather gear (which were rarely waterproof)), temporary green ear defender things (not soundproof), bush jackets (not fashionable), long white socks, long white shorts, white shoes with no tread, stiff collars (incredibly difficult to put on with a tie, especially a bow tie), trench coats, fearnought suits (i.e. firefighting suits (which were always wet when undertaking firefighting training)) and respirators (not for use by anyone with a narrow face).

There were usually two laundrymen on a frigate or destroyer. In most of my ships they were known as No. 1 and No. 2, and typically they used to be from China or Hong Kong. Depending on one's role in the ship, one might muster a smile from them or not. They tended to live in the dhobey shack (a compartment at the aft end of the ship) and eat their own food, and were rarely seen outside of the dhobey shack other than when they went ashore to a casino during port visits. Once, onboard HMS *Endurance*, alongside in the Falklands on the day after Chinese New Year, the following pipe was made: **'D'you hear there, the laundry is closed for the day.'**

On hearing this pipe, the Captain told the OOD that such pipes are unhelpful and it is always important to inform the ship's company the reason for such surprising announcements. The OOD duly relayed this message to the QM. A few seconds later the following pipe was made: **'D'you hear there, the laundry is closed today because the laundryman is pissed out of his head. That is all.'**

The Captain was disappointed with this pipe.

Personally, I found the laundrymen to be cheerful and helpful, but given that I (as LO) technically provided them with dhobey dust (laundry powder), this might account for cordial relations. The MEO technically provided them with steam and power. The Captain was in charge. Hence we three were all liked.

The presence of dhobeymen removes the need for sailors to personally clean their uniform and civvies while at sea. However, they are still required to clean their uniform when they join the RN at HMS *Raleigh*. For some reason, recruits entering HMS *Raleigh* are also told to bring ironing boards with them despite there being an abundance of ironing boards fixed to the floor in the accommodation blocks. On one occasion, I witnessed a recruit arrive having brought his ironing board from Carmarthen using three trains. It was taken from him by a member of staff upon arrival and never seen again.

One can typically guess a person's status in their ship even when in civilian clothing. Junior ratings will tend to reflect the fashion of the day, and some will wear clothing designed for the summer irrespective of where the ship is berthed. Some may wear a football shirt or Union Jack shorts. This is not always allowed, and after the Iraq War in 2003, sailors going ashore in the Gulf region were directed not to wear Union Jack shorts. We were therefore slightly surprised that, when a couple of fellow officers and I visited a hotel in Muscat, our CO emerged from the changing area wearing a t-shirt which had the following depicted on it:

Front: 'HMS NOTTINGHAM, SNFM 1996'

Back: A pair of Union Jack Y-fronts with the following written underneath: 'It was Pants'

Maybe he didn't read Daily Orders …

CPOs will reflect the fashion of the year of their parents' birth, or will proceed ashore wearing golf attire despite the fact that it is a working day. Some may wear denim jeans with a crease irrespective of whether the dhobeyman has placed it there or not. POs will be somewhere in between, but when alongside they are probably in their mess on the first night in anyway (which may result in a beer ban), or will have been banned from going ashore. Officers will wear dog robbers or, if feeling very daring, planters. They may, in a desperate move to become liberated and reveal their true self or be popular, smuggle jeans in a bag and get changed once ashore. Cadets at BRNC would often smuggle denim clothing out of the College in order to visit Torquay or the Groin Exchange.

Wearing uniform and headgear (i.e. a cap) necessitates saluting an officer, and for them to return the salute. Standards of saluting differ. The Army, RAF, RN Gunners and members of the Royal Marines Band Service tend to take great pride in their salute. The quality of sailors' salutes varies; some might go to great lengths to avoid saluting an officer, and indeed an officer might go to great lengths to avoid being saluted.

As a sub-lieutenant I was once laughed at by a submariner lieutenant for saluting him. As Captain of HMS *Raleigh*, walking not far away from an accommodation block, I was saluted by a recruit who was not wearing his beret. He realized as soon as his hand touched

WHAT IS A FLIGHT DECK ACTUALLY FOR ANYWAY?

his head that his beret was missing. In a state of worry he said, 'Oh shit, Sir, sorry ... what should I do?' I told him to run quickly to his block to fetch his beret before a grumpy CPO or warrant officer saw him. Unfortunately, he was intercepted shortly afterwards by a CPO. I felt guilty.

'D'you hear there, flight deck sports are about to commence on the flight deck. All are welcome!'

Before exploring this pipe, it is important to note that submarines do not have flight decks, and neither do minehunters. Aircraft carriers obviously have flight decks, but they are very big. Frigates and destroyers, however, have relatively small spaces to accommodate aircraft, and they are typically the size of a tennis court. They also have no hard perimeter; instead they have the sea, and given that the ship is invariably moving, any ball lost over the side is likely to end up like Wilson from *Castaway*. The surface of the flight deck is rough: not something upon which one would wish to fall. There

is also a metal grid in the middle of the flight deck to which the helicopter attaches itself when being recovered (i.e. landing) on the ship. So flight deck sports are played in a confined area resembling a tennis court which is moving and beyond which one cannot reclaim a lost ball. It is, even without the playing of sport, a relatively hazardous area.

Nonetheless, life at sea can become mundane, and the boredom can be overcome by participating in flight deck sports. These are occasions in which messdecks compete against each other. In reality, flight deck sports are designed to let the chiefs' mess overcome their age by winning through foul means, brute force or bribery. There are a number of different flight deck sports.

Brighter cricket – the source of the name is unclear, but it involves an orthodox, and fairly old, cricket bat, a ball made out of masking tape, and a set of wickets. It tends to follow the pattern of cricket with some variations. Once the ball has been bowled to the batter, the batter runs to one side of the flight deck and back to the stumps irrespective of whether they have hit the ball or not. They will continue to do this, progressively flailing the bat in a meaningless manner until either they collapse or hit the ball and are caught or the ball hits the wickets.

Flight deck hockey – flight deck hockey is very similar to professional ice hockey, although the levels of violence are far greater than those in the North American Hockey Leagues. There is no official umpire – it is either Clubz or one or all of the chiefs. The event tends to be won by the chiefs' mess. Typically it is also an opportunity for anybody to legitimately hack lumps out of the officers. As in Brighter Cricket, the equipment is rudimentary, with little or no protective kit available. The chance of damage to shins is significant, although this can be partially mitigated by using three-week-old newspapers or magazines under one's socks.

Bucket ball – bucket ball is a variation of netball and basketball. Two teams endeavour to place a ball made out of masking tape into a bucket. The bucket is placed on the head of a teammate (usually a junior member of each messdeck who can be shouted at for not moving their head to catch the ball), who stands on a chair while the ship rolls from side to side. A rudimentary risk assessment will be made prior to standing on the chair.

Tug of war – there is very little variation to standard tug of war except that rather than face each other the teams may be placed side by side, and that the rope is pulled through shackles attached to the deck. On one occasion in HMS *Aurora*, 3L Mess (mainly young ROs and chefs) were thrashing the senior rates to great cheers of joy from the ship's company. This cheering subsided when it became clear that 3L Mess had secured their end of the rope to a bollard on the Starboard Waist. Sadly, they were disqualified.

Horse racing – live animals are rarely carried onboard, although one mess did abscond with a live monkey many years ago, and once discovered by the First Lieutenant it was placed in a small boat on Health and Safety grounds and cast away with water and provisions (way before my time, I might add). However, replica horses are used at horse racing nights, based on very strict betting rules.

Flight deck sports are likely to cause injury. If an MO is embarked, and if sober or not playing uckers, they may treat the casualty or, more likely, and arguably fortuitously, the casualty will be treated by the POMA instead.

'The Captain is requested to come to the Bridge at the rush.'
This pipe is politely asking the Captain to come to the Bridge very quickly so that they can take the blame given that the ship is about to crash. The pipe, while delivered with courtesy, is actually masking an emerging issue that really does require the Captain's attention. The 'at the rush' bit is the giveaway line, and it is likely to spur the Captain, and indeed the rest of the ship's company, into action.

At sea, in peacetime, the Captain will tend to remain on the Bridge or in their cabin immediately below or behind the Bridge so that they can be contacted immediately. However, occasionally the Captain will stray further from the Bridge, and that can be either to meet members of the ship's company who may ordinarily not operate in the vicinity of their cabin or Bridge, or to attend flight deck barbecues or flight deck sports.

OOWs are trained to tell the Captain of the following incidents:

1. The sun has come up (stating the amount of cloud in the sky).
2. The sun has gone down, and the navigation lights on the ship are working, as is the radar.
3. Another ship is within 100 miles of our ship (well, less than that, but it does mean that the Captain is called frequently, especially at night).
4. Something is broken.

On occasions when the Captain is called to the Bridge at the rush, it is usually because another ship has actually come very close to the ship, or will do so unless evasive action is taken. However, taking evasive action, or not, has consequences: either legal consequences based on internationally recognized *Rules of the Road* (a highway code for mariners), or because it might require a change of course or speed to achieve a particular objective. Therefore, although the OOW is capable of making decisions, there are occasions when deviations from particular routines or plans require the Captain's counsel or authority. Put another way, the Captain is piped to the Bridge in order to tell the OOW to tell the QM to move the rudder. By this time, the incident has become the Captain's responsibility rather than that of the OOW. Thus, if in doubt, call the Captain! That being said, calling the Captain might make them grumpy – a lose-lose situation.

'D'you hear there, the flight deck BBQ will commence at 1800. Rig: Banyan Rig.'

Occasionally, to break the monotony of long passages at sea, and to give the chefs the evening off, the ship will have a barbecue on the flight deck. In reality, the chefs do not have an evening off as they will cook off most of the meat to ensure people do not die of food poisoning. All unnecessary items, such as the helicopter (which some consider has no place on the flight deck and really should be back at the Royal Naval Air Station in Yeovilton), will be removed. The

WHAT IS A FLIGHT DECK ACTUALLY FOR ANYWAY?

WAFUs' clickclick beds (i.e. deckchairs), usually kept for day time use only, will be a priceless commodity at the barbecue. The Flight might even move to Alert 45+ (i.e. a state of reduced readiness) ensuring that they get even more than eight hours in bed.

Most people enter into the spirit of the flight deck barbecue. Many will wear outlandish barbecue clothing; the CPOs will wear their usual run ashore rig. Officers will wear shorts, and some will also have socks and sandals. The attendees will also try to eat their food using a paper plate and a flimsy plastic fork (a skill honed during Action Messing at OST). This merriment and all of one company gathering will be accompanied by popular music (Sandie Shaw or the Beach Boys).

The cunning CANMAN will use this as an opportunity to shift out-of-date beer, which will be stowed either in a cool box or a bin. I am not sure how the sailors' three tins per day rule is followed on these occasions.

Saturday nights at sea may often cause one's thoughts to turn to home; hence, to relieve the boredom and sadness, a film might follow the barbecue. A white sheet will be draped across the hangar door to form a very basic and low-definition screen. The viewers will then attempt to listen to the sound of the movie over the noise of the ship's engines, and occasional vibration of the deck. The lucky few (i.e. WAFUs) will have their own deck chairs, while others will have to sit on the deck, and take turns deciding which hand to place on the deck before it burns or becomes imprinted and dented with camrex paint. Only two thirds of the ship's company will watch the film at any one time; the rest will be tabbing on the quarterdeck next to gash bags stowed in a cargo net. A firm favourite is *The Cruel Sea*, based on Nicholas Monsarrat's novel of the same name, which became a classic wartime film. Depicting life onboard a Second World War corvette through the eyes of three members of the ship's company, it graphically illustrates the impact of life on those at sea, as well as the families at home, during wartime, thereby demonstrating that, irrespective of rank and status, many of the experiences were largely the same for all, though in subtly different ways; essentially reflecting the 'all of one company' nature of life at sea. It also brings to life the consequences of losing one's ship and the raw nature of survival at sea.

Although this film is presented on a one-dimensional sheet affixed to a hangar door, significant effort is expended in simulating the unpleasant nature of life on an open Bridge in a cold and stormy Atlantic Ocean. Some viewers might wear woolly jumpers and pusser's (flasher) Burberry raincoats, but their experience will be greatly enhanced by our good friends the senior rates throwing buckets of cold water over the viewers at various points of the movie. During mealtimes at sea, the presence of sausages on the menu in the Wardroom is likely to lead to the uttering of the phrase, 'Snorkers, Good Oh.' One might also recall various points during the movie when the BM hollers onto 2 Deck (in a northern accent), 'Hands to Stations for leaving 'arbour, Special Sea Dutymen close oop'. That is, of course, a pipe (which, of course, those non-matelot readers will now instinctively understand).

In the Wardroom, the First Lieutenant might invite the Captain into the mess. Having had a tin of beer or a sherry, the Captain will be offered the most còmfortable chair. The more junior officers will sit on the deck. The MEO will be removed for wearing overalls. Everyone will have a choc ice.

Back in the early 2000s, prior to sailing, one mess chose which film they would watch on the first Saturday night of the deployment. They chose *Team America*, which was billed as a comedy involving puppets (similar to *Thunderbirds*). One officer, knowing the first Saturday can be quite difficult, bought the DVD for his wife and children to watch at home so they could all watch it at the same time despite being apart. He watched the film in growing fear and sadness when it became clear that *Team America* is not suitable for children! It did not merit Naval Personnel and Family Services (NPFS)[*] being involved, but it may have required a phone call home during the first run ashore in Gibraltar. Unfortunately, the phone call might not have taken place as planned given that his 'phonecall run' oppos thought it was a good idea to have 'a sharpener' in the Donkey's Flip Flop

---

[*] In every organization and branch in the RN, names/titles are changed on a routine basis, and so although 'NPFS' is no longer called by this name anymore, by the time this book is published it will have probably reverted to the name 'NPFS'!

WHAT IS A FLIGHT DECK ACTUALLY FOR ANYWAY?

(aka The Horseshoe public house). Fortunately, they made it back to the ship 45 minutes before the commencement of the Rock Race* at 0500 the following day.

As an alternative to flight deck sports, the following pipe might be made: **'D'you hear there, the flight deck village fete will take place at 1300. All are welcome.'**

The reader will now be aware that as well as being an important place to launch and recover a helicopter (unless it is broken or the Flight are tired), the flight deck is a versatile part of the ship. It can be the location of a reception with sophisticated water features and a fully stocked bar; it can be a music venue; it can be the scene of people departing and arriving onboard in various states; it can be a sports location; it can be a fitness suite; it can be a cinema; and it can be a horse race venue. It can also be made into an idyllic village green on which summer fetes can be held.

On such occasions, typically on a long passage in sunny climes, the ship's company will have a well-earned afternoon off (unless they are on watch) in order to take part in the 'village fete'. Various stances and stalls are sponsored by each mess, including placing officers in stocks; splat the rat; banging nails into pieces of wood; throwing custard pies at the First Lieutenant (i.e. the XO) or Buffer†; an extremely basic fruit machine where the only resemblance to a real fruit machine was a handle (broom), and the fruit combinations would be drawn out of a box randomly by sailors (or perhaps not randomly, depending on whether people liked you or not); a raffle (prizes might range from being Captain for the Day to conducting rounds in the cabins of heads of department); and Bruce Forsyth's

---

* The Rock Race is an infamous tradition in the RN when during a visit to Gibraltar, personnel are invited to literally run from the bottom of the Rock of Gibraltar to the top. It takes place early in the morning (i.e. to avoid disruption to traffic). Some compete to win the race, others undertake the race for charity and some do it because they have no choice (i.e. Officers Under Training). Most are glad just to get to the top of the Rock!

† Chief Bosun's Mate (senior Seaman Specialist) – typically quite grumpy.

Play Your Cards Right (in which someone, usually a bearded CPO, would dress as a glamorous assistant).

'Standby for evening rounds!'
This pipe will have been preceded (approximately one hour beforehand) by the following pipe: **'Out pipes, clean up messdecks, heads and bathrooms for evening rounds.'**

For some, these are discretionary pipes. Officers and senior ratings have the discretion to ignore them as they are not subjected to rounds (except for OST and Captain's Rounds – at that point officers wear gleaming white overalls, and it makes them feel at one with the lower deck sailors on an annual basis).

For the rest of the ship's company it involves cleaning heads and bathrooms, messdecks and passageways. It also involves choosing somebody to report the mess to the inspecting officer for evening rounds. This is learned at HMS *Raleigh* and BRNC.

Reporting a mess for evening rounds for the first time is daunting. It sometimes leads to the rating forgetting who and where they are, and also might cause them to salute like Benny Hill with the left hand.

On one occasion at HMS *Raleigh*, the Captain took part in the rounds route. Having arrived at the messdeck with the Commander and Joss in tow, the rating stood petrified and speechless in front of the Captain. Eventually the Joss said, 'Come on lad, don't leave the Captain stood there to attention all day.' The rating, fresh from drill training, nervously replied, 'Captain ... stand at ease.' That is a safeguard dit!

Rounds at *Raleigh* and BRNC incorporate microscopic elements of detail, commencing with a recruit or cadet's personal kit. Shirts, trousers and underwear are to be clean and pressed into the size of an A4 piece of paper (in order to generate the discipline of using a confined area of personal space). Boots are to be clean and highly polished. Many moons ago, trainers or daps (possessing absolutely no element of physical support to the feet) would be spotlessly white in order to climb a mangled rope the following day.

WHAT IS A FLIGHT DECK ACTUALLY FOR ANYWAY?

Beyond clothing, the messdeck itself is inspected for cleanliness and serviceability of lights, hatches and escape equipment. Basins will need to be dry (despite leaking taps), and plugs will need to be coiled neatly despite the chain not being affixed to the basin. Immediately prior to the inspecting officer's arrival, air freshener is usually sprayed to either enhance the impact of the cleaning or create a perception that some effort has been expended to clean the compartment.

At sea, the standards of cleanliness and detail of the inspections are not as granular as during initial training or OST, but they are, nonetheless, required and take place daily unless it is Christmas Day. The XO will usually undertake the rounds accompanied by the Joss or Regulating Petty Officer (RPO) and the BM. The BM will sound a continuous pipe during the XO's procession throughout 2 Deck and into each messdeck. Upon arrival in the messdeck, the occupants of the messdeck will usually be sitting in the mess square looking innocent and bored. The XO might attempt to engage the sailors in conversation. Some find this easier than others. The XO's questions and comments will be met either with stunned silence or with drips (moaning) about the food, the ship's routine or the ship's programme.

Once rounds are complete the XO will provide an 'Evening Sitrep' pipe, along the following lines:

[XO's comments in **bold**, sailors' likely comments *in italics*]

'D'you hear there, First Lieutenant speaking, with an evening sitrep ... *Here we go.*

Rounds this evening were genuinely good, but greater attention needs to be made to overhead lights and in the corners of flats where dust can easily gather. Keep up the good work.

Well done to the WEs' mess for putting on the barbecue this evening ... *They didn't actually cook it, the chefs did.*

Well done for the Warfare and Engineering Teams for yesterday's RAS in very difficult conditions ... *What about the chefs?!*

As you know, Admiral Jellicoe will be visiting while alongside this week. He will very much look forward to meeting you and hearing your views

about the Navy. Please give him the usual Battleaxe welcome ... *I bet he doesn't bring any newspapers!*

The Captain obviously provided the disappointing news today that our planned trip to Jamaica has been replaced by a visit to the Falklands. The Visit Liaison Team will be working hard to provide a cracking visit to the Falklands, and I know they are looking to arrange sports fixtures, and a visit to the local Royal British Legion. It promises to be a good run ashore and a great reward for all of your hard work. It will be a busy visit with a cocktail party, reception and children's parties ... *That's no shore leave for the chefs then!*

Finally, I am sure you would all like to join me in congratulating the Captain on winning £5,000 in the Sports Lottery. Well done, Ma'am ... *Creep!*

Have a good evening. That is all! ...' *Have a good evening stuck here going to the Falklands instead of Jamaica.*

Day 47

Never Run Out of Beer ... or Loo Rolls

LOCATION: AT SEA

'Toilet rolls are now ready for collection from No. 1 Naval Store.'
To the untrained eye this is either a pipe that requires no translation or a pipe that is rarely, if ever, necessary given that toilet rolls are an obvious consumable item of Naval Stores which do not require any form of particular control. However, if one were to run out of toilet roll at sea, this would present a problem, and having nearly done so in the Indian Ocean, I considered it helpful to discuss what this pipe means!

In many ways this pipe was unique to the Type 22 frigate HMS *Chatham*. After I joined HMS *Chatham* in April 2003, the ship departed the Arabian Gulf (in which it had played a key role in the Iraq War) and then proceeded to the Indian Ocean to find terrorists. During this time, I was disappointed to be briefed that we were running perilously low on toilet rolls. The ship was due to meet a consignment of spares and supplies in Bahrain, but unfortunately it did not make that rendezvous, meaning that there was a shortage of toilet rolls. Sadly, I was only informed after sailing. This not only prompted me to ask my caterers to review the menu (and remove items which might otherwise lead to freer flowing bowel movements), but also required me to ensure that any remaining toilet rolls would be closely rationed for the remainder of my time as LO. Fortunately, we managed to divert a German replenishment ship some 2,000 miles to top us up. How we laughed!

Less fortunately, by the time we discovered the shortage, the ship was stationed off East Africa, which in 2003 was not an area conducive to port visits or helicopter mercy missions. I do recall at the time that the Captain directed that his own personal toilet roll be placed in his safe. I did the same, I am ashamed to say. I still have one of the German toilet rolls at home as a reminder of that fateful time!

In some ships, the issue of toilet rolls might lead to the following pipe: **'D'you hear there, toilet tissues are being issued from the toilet tissue store.'**[*]

Fortunately, the Navy is good at learning from mistakes, and when officers undertake particular pieces of training at key moments of their career there is, for a navy with such a history as the Royal Navy, an abundance of stories and lessons from which they can learn. From that moment, at the Logistics School, future LOs were told of the time one of their predecessors nearly ran out of toilet rolls in the Indian Ocean. Somehow, I went on to command the Logistics School, and blushed when the story was told … over and over again.

'The Operations Officer is requested to take a shore telephone call from the MCO.'

This pipe tends to happen, on average, eight times per day and is typically timed just as the Operations Officer (known as the 'Ops Officer') has finished writing the Longcast. The Longcast provides a forecast of the ship's future programme. It gives sufficient detail for personnel to forecast where the ship is going, and therefore when to plan certain activities such as fuelling, store ship and runs ashore. This particular phone call is likely to render fruitless the time expended on writing the Longcast.

Though less so in the present day Navy, the ability to make or receive telephone calls external to the ship will still often be limited to the Captain's cabin, the MCO or possibly the Bridge. The Bridge also has the ability to communicate by voice with nearby ships using a VHF Radio. Therefore, those personnel needing to communicate

---

[*] It's a play on alliteration (try saying it fast).

with shoreside authorities many hundreds of miles from the UK will usually need to visit the MCO.

Having been piped to the MCO, the Ops Officer will wearily climb or descend the ladder to the MCO. Noting that the method of communicating with shoreside authorities is primarily through moving satellites from a moving ship, the quality of the telephone call might not be reliable, and it is highly likely that by the time they have arrived in the MCO and picked up the phone, the phone line will be dead. In anticipation that the shoreside authority will immediately seek to reconnect with the ship, it would be prudent for the Ops Officer to remain in the vicinity of the MCO rather than walk back to their cabin. Eventually, as time ticks by without a call back, the Ops Officer will return to their cabin, at which point they are likely to be piped back to the MCO. The inconsistent connectivity of the satellite communication might result in the phone line often going down at a critical moment of a conversation.

Modern communications have enabled more frequent telephone calls of an official and unofficial nature to be made for ships at sea. However, until approximately 25 years ago, most people could only phone family and friends when the ship had come alongside after a few weeks at sea. This entailed going to a local phone box and making a call on the side of a busy road using a pre-charged card bought from a kiosk; alternatively, a phone call could be made to the ship from the UK.

The latter occasion could lead to the following pipes:
'Cdr Harris is requested to dial zero.'
'Lt Rollason dial 78150 [or 151].'
'Wtr Bearcroft, shore telephone call, Captain's cabin.'
There are three points to make, one for each of the above pipes.

Officers of the rank of lieutenant commander and above are 'requested' to go to places to do particular things. This is polite but, some would say, unnecessary.

Lt Rollason on this occasion is lucky as she is going to take a call on one of the new phones installed on HM ships. These new phones were initially the size of a small car and their ring tone sounded like the start of the theme tune to *Dallas*.

On this occasion, Wtr Bearcroft has had her telephone call unintentionally plugged through to the Captain's cabin as opposed to the Gangway or HQ1. Such an occasion is rare as the Captain's cabin is, as one will understand, exclusively for the Captain's own use. This particular pipe will have therefore probably led to a degree of embarrassment for Wtr Bearcroft and, unless the Captain is of a kind disposition, a degree of irritation from the Captain.

There are occasions when other members of the ship's company are given access to the Captain's cabin. At Christmas or as a raffle prize another member of the ship's company can be the Captain for the day, having use of the bath (if installed) and the fridge.

Other than for these rare occasions, the Captain's cabin is exclusively for the Captain's use. Most ships, except minor war vessels or submarines, will have both a Captain's day and a Captain's night cabin. In the day cabin, there is usually a sofa with gaudy flower patterns, a comfy chair which unhelpfully slides across the carpet when the ship rolls, a dining table, a desk and computer. Various books will also be contained behind a glass panel, and a telescope and a barometer would be placed on the bulkhead. Pictures might adorn the wooden MFI bulkheads, and there will be items associated with the ship's affiliated town or city. If the Captain has children they might have a photograph of a loved one, and they might have their children's drawings on the bulkhead. As an officer under training, I struggled not to titter at the drawing of my captain, who appeared to take the form of a muppet. Maybe that distraction is why I failed my Young Officer's Dummy Fleetboard when he asked me questions (although, to be fair, there were a few gaps in my knowledge).

The cabin also has a helpful hatch through which cutlery can be passed into the scullery and through which the Captain might talk to the steward. Unlike most other members of the ship's company, who the Captain will usually refer to by their role (e.g. Buffer, Chippy, Pusser, Doc, Bish, No. 1, Engines) or by their rate and surname, many captains refer to their steward by their first name or by their nickname.

The night cabin will contain a comfy bed, a scuttle (i.e. a window) and a set of heads and a shower (and maybe a bath).

Throughout the day the Captain might receive various visitors, and only *in extremis* will the Captain order people to come to their cabin. One such pipe might be:

'Duty WE Senior Rate, Captain's cabin.'

Or

'The WEO is requested to report to the Captain's cabin.'

This pipe is likely to be made in the event of the Captain's personal television not working. There are a number of reasons why the television might not be working. It might be because the satellite is moving and the ship is moving concurrently (an issue affecting the whole ship). It might be because it was not plugged in after the steward vacuumed (not hoovered! (see page 45)) the cabin. Or it might be user error (likely).

The need to order the WEO to attend and fix the problem is comparable to using a hammer to crack a nut. That being said, it is likely that this will expose the WEO's experience gap in television fault finding. It is more likely that asking the WEO to fix the television is mainly aimed at providing entertainment for the Captain at the WEO's expense!

Generally, the duty WE Senior Rate will be the optimum solution, and upon arrival in the Captain's cabin, they will soon determine that the batteries in the remote control are flat, and will need changing. Unfortunately, the Captain's own efforts to rectify the issue (rather than wake the duty WE Senior Rate during the Dogs), will have led to their reprogramming the television and the DVD player. The Duty WE Senior Rate will then have to retune all of the audio visual equipment in the Captain's cabin. This process will be repeated on a regular basis throughout the deployment.

'D'you hear there, personnel are to keep clear of the for'd Seawolf launcher. Launcher may train and elevate without warning.'

The upper deck of a warship contains a number of items which are hazardous. This includes ropes, wires, hatches, doors, exhausts, sirens, sailors(!), radars and weapons. This pipe is warning the ship's company that functionality tests are being undertaken on one of the Seawolf missile launchers (see SOCs pipe, page 45), and that it may move (quickly) without warning. Thus, personnel are to take care.

Missile firings are a relatively rare occurrence in peacetime. Missiles are expensive, and if you are lucky enough to see them being fired, be careful not to blink or you might miss it.

Gun firings are far more regular, and vary in size and sound. A frigate's or destroyer's main gun is positioned at the bow and is used to provide naval gunfire support, or naval fires, in support of personnel (i.e. Royal Marines or British Army) ashore; this was undertaken, with precision and bravery, by ships on the gunlines during Operation *Corporate* in the Falklands conflict in 1982, and in Operation *Telic*, Iraq, in 2003. The gun also has a secondary function of engaging surface targets (i.e. other ships). In the Operations Room several personnel will be very excited during gunnery drills, most notably the Principal Warfare Officer (Above Water) (PWO(A)), the Gunnery/Missile Ratings and the WEs (especially if the gun actually works). The interaction of the net (the radio circuit) is likely to go along the following lines:

4.5 Indirect Bombardment, select new target. Tanks in the Open. Five salvoes, fire for effect ... 4.5 Engage!

At the point 'Engage', the following might happen:

1. The gun will fire a shell (very loudly) followed by the smell of cordite in the ship.
2. The gun will stop working.
3. Someone will shout the word 'BANG' (if deliberately conducting drills without firing the weapon).

On occasions when undertaking such firings, for exercise or for real world events, the ship might embark a member of the Royal Artillery or Royal Marines, known as the Naval Gunfire Liaison Officer (NGLO), who would assist and advise on gunnery activity and on any necessary adjustments or corrections to the firing orders and calculations. If the NGLO had not been to sea before, they might be invited to settle their mess bill before departing the ship. Additionally, they might be invited to settle their bunk light bill. If the NGLO was lucky enough to be allocated a bunk or cabin it is likely that they will have used their tiny bunk light at some stage, and, in jest, they will be charged a usage fee for their light. Many might assume this is a legitimate charge. I am unsure whether anybody actually paid it: doubtful, but you never know. Additionally, fresh faces unfamiliar with life at sea might be seen shining torches at the emergency luminescent arrows on the deck and bulkheads in order to ensure that the arrows are 'fully charged'. I never did this, but I did visit the Buffer to ask for 'a long weight'; and waited for a considerable period of time.

Although a ship might visit a fully functioning firing range (such as Cape Wrath) to conduct firing exercises, it might also be possible to conduct shorter range firing exercises for small weaponry (close range weapons) while at sea by placing a large inflatable red target, known as the Killer Tomato, in the water, or by towing a floating target behind the ship. This was known as a Larne Target (and resembled a metal grill construction). Again, it would not be unusual to ask naive young sailors if they wanted to volunteer to become Larne Target coxswains.

'D'you hear there, all volunteers for Larne Target coxswain training are to muster on the quarterdeck at 1500.'

Thereupon, the volunteers would be dressed in protective clothing to enable them to perform their spurious/false duty.

'Man overboard, man overboard, man overboard, man overboard starboard side. Away seaboat, away swimmer of the watch!'

Irrespective of the ultimate requirement to engage with one of the King's enemies at sea, life on a warship is dangerous. There are many hazards which might be simply summarized by being in a tin box in which there are flammable fuels, weapons and ammunition, and surrounded by the sea. While the chances of a member of the ship's company falling overboard are low, it can happen, and an RAS, for example, is a particular hazardous evolution in which the chances of a person falling overboard are heightened.

There are some evolutions (exercises) which are more frequently exercised than others; man overboard and fires or flood exercises are the most frequent. In the case of a man overboard exercise, this pipe will be prefixed by the following: **'For exercise, for exercise, for exercise, man overboard, man overboard, man overboard …'**

Typically, a man overboard (MOB) exercise will be conducted at a critical point of preparing lunch, causing the ship to manoeuvre violently, and making the chefs sad (see page 62).

The pipe itself is alerting the ship's company that one of their shipmates has fallen overboard. It is also ordering nominated personnel to prepare the seaboat (or one of the seaboats)* to be lowered into the water to recover the person, and, concurrently, for the nominated Swimmer of the Watch (SOW) to dress in a

---

* A seaboat is a powerful rigid inflatable boat. As well as being used to recover personnel who have fallen overboard, it may be used for boarding operations, landing personnel ashore, collecting mail and acting as Sharkwatch during 'Hands to Bathe' (see page 96).

waterproof multifab suit*. The SOW, once dressed in the suit, will proceed to a point on the upper deck, and will have a line (rope) attached to them. Once the signal has been given, the SOW will jump into the sea as an alternative method to the seaboat of recovering the MOB. Nominated personnel will also muster on the upper deck to handle the line attached to the SOW and they will help pull the SOW back onboard. It is hoped that the MOB will have been sighted shortly after falling into the water, and personnel will gather on the Bridge wing to physically sight and point to the MOB. Lifebuoys will have been dropped into the water as soon as it becomes clear that someone has fallen overboard. The chart will also be marked (known as 'marking the plot') to record the location of the ship at the point the MOB took place. All of those activities should enable the ship to swiftly record, observe and recover the MOB, noting that the temperature of the water, the shock of falling into the water or the sea state will place the MOB in peril. The OOW will conduct initial manoeuvring to enable the ship quickly and effectively to return to the position where the person fell overboard. This is known as the Williamson Turn, and it is taught to all officer cadets at BRNC from the very earliest days at the College, irrespective of whether they are Warfare Officers or not (except chaplains, who will walk to the MOB).

At BRNC, cadets will also be taught bends and hitches (ropework), navigation, how to march, how to eat (but not to eat with a fruit knife and fork), how to speak, how to write, how to dance (a long time ago), how to arrive 5 minutes before 5 minutes before (deliberately repeated) the time of a meeting; known as the 5-Minute Rule. If cadets are late arriving at Sandquay, the College's area for boat training, which is several hundred feet, and steps, beneath the College, they might become acquainted with Sid the Shackle and have to run back up to the top of the hill with Sid as a reminder of the need for punctuality.

---

* Which may actually not be waterproof anymore.

There are occasions where it is entirely acceptable for personnel to be in the sea, such as after the following pipe: **'D'you hear there, First Lieutenant speaking. In view of the very clement weather today, the ship has stopped in the water and, for those who wish, this is a good opportunity to take a dip, therefore*** **... hands to bathe, hands to bathe.'**

As the First Lieutenant has stated, for those who wish, there are occasional opportunities for personnel to swim in the middle of the sea. For those who, like the author, struggle with their feet not being able to touch the bottom, this is not an invitation likely to be accepted, though one might wish to 'tick it off the taskbook† of life' at least once. Those brave souls who undertake 'Hands to Bathe' face three perils. Firstly, there is the chance that someone might accidentally start or stop underwater equipment, such as propulsion or sonars, although the ship will have standard 'Shiphaz' procedures that should ensure that all appropriate equipment is isolated. Secondly, they face the peril of actually jumping into the water (which, for those afraid of heights, might be a challenge), followed by the need to return onboard. Unless they are serving in an amphibious assault ship, which has its own dock and ramp that can form a rudimentary and very hard beach, they will have to clamber up a cargo net rigged over the ship's side. Unless they have taken a dip wearing a pair of trainers, this will be painful. It may be appropriate to pose a question to the reader at this point, and consider what the third peril might be? Seagull‡? Whale? Shark? These are indeed potential hazards to matelots in the water. In order to deal with the threat potentially posed by a shark,

---

* Never forget the key 'therefore' word!
† Junior sailors wishing to qualify for the next higher rate and eventually become selected for promotion have to undertake a taskbook. The taskbook includes various professional and also management and leadership tasks that one has to undertake, and have signed off by a competent senior. Officers under training also have a taskbook. I managed to have my flashing light/morse code task signed off successfully by a yeoman who liked chocolate Hobnobs.
‡ Known to matelots as 'shitehawks'.

a sailor will undertake the duty of 'Sharkwatch', and will be armed with a rifle either from the seaboat or from the Bridge wing, ready to shoot a shark. For the benefit of the circumspect reader, this is actually a safeguard aspect of 'Hands to Bathe'; yes, there is a matelot with a gun ready to shoot a shark which might swim among a group of sailors splashing around in the water. Unlike soldiers, sailors rarely fire rifles, so this in itself might be a worse peril than that posed by a predator of the deep. There are, therefore, on reflection, four perils associated with 'Hands to Bathe'.

Incidentally, Sharkwatch has two meanings: either for 'Hands to Bathe' or when, during times of a heightened domestic threat, one sailor is assigned as a sober member of a group of sailors on a run ashore who should remain alert to any suspicious activity.

After 'Hands to Bathe', and before the ship sails to its next location, all personnel will be mustered by mess to ensure that all are actually onboard.

In the event of a sailor suspected of being missing while at sea (because they have either been eaten by a shark during 'Hands to Bathe' or fallen over the side during an RAS or while collecting a cricket bat from the sea during Brighter Cricket), the ship will undertake 'Op *Thimblehunt*'. This will require a thorough search of the ship in order to find the missing person.

Fortunately, all members of the Royal Navy are required to demonstrate a basic level of swimming aptitude before they pass out of HMS *Raleigh*, BRNC or the Commando Training Centre, Lympstone[*] – though I suspect the Royal Marine Swimming Test is more arduous and requires a bootneck (i.e. Royal Marine) to carry another bootneck on their back. This is known as the Royal Navy Swimming Test (RNST), and once passed, a sailor's Service documentation will be annotated 'PRNST'. The RNST involves wearing a damp set of overalls. The sailor will then jump into a swimming pool and swim two lengths of the pool, tread water for 2 minutes, and then climb out of the water unaided. For some reason, officers were also required to dive for a brick. I never understood

---

[*] The training establishment for the Royal Marines.

why an officer would need to demonstrate an ability to dive 10ft for a brick whereas a rating would not. In actual fact, I would have assumed it would be the other way around, and the rating would have to perform the more arduous task, and maybe dive to rescue an officer's signet ring. While one might think this comment is in jest, I am aware that one senior officer, having just used the heads and dropped his comb into the toilet, asked his steward to retrieve the comb. This is not only an entirely inappropriate demand, but it would almost certainly lead to the officer being on the receiving end of Stewards 9s at some stage.[*]

Other occasions when personnel might be in the sea next to the ship might be when deploying the ship's divers to inspect the ship's hull, or the time when at least one CO decided to water ski while attached to the ship. My understanding was that he was not particularly well liked, which probably made his venture all the more risky.

---

[*] No. 9 punishment is a formal summary punishment which might be ordered by a CO or XO. It entails extra work and drill outside of the normal working day (0800–1600). It is shortened to '9s'. Stewards 9s or Chefs 9s do not involve extra work and drill, but it might be used to describe how a hard-done-by steward or chef might choose to seek some form of retribution.

Day 48

Giblets and Haggis

LOCATION: AT SEA

'D'you hear there, CBRNDC circuit training will take place this morning at 0900. All offwatch personnel are to muster on the flight deck at 0900. That is all.'

All personnel are trained in aspects of serving in a Chemical, Biological, Radiation and Nuclear environment and Damage Control (i.e. CBRNDC) during their initial naval training (i.e. the initial training undertaken by each person when they join the RN (either at HMS *Raleigh* or BRNC), and prior to going to sea. They also receive further training if undertaking OST or, when deployed, might undertake continuity training delivered by specially trained members of the ship's company, known as 'Q's. This continuity training is known as circuit training, and while it is not related to physical training, the concept is similar: personnel are split into groups and visit certain locations in the ship in which they undertake various CBRNDC activities; typically these involve firefighting, leak stopping and pumping and flooding, casualty handling, and upper deck and personal cleansing in a nuclear or chemical environment. The most likely skills and experience to be deployed in a real-time environment are based on firefighting, leak stopping and pumping and flooding, or casualty handling. These are ever-present aspects of life at sea irrespective of peacetime or wartime. Fires can range from small 'gash bag'* fires to larger and far more dangerous fires in engine and machinery spaces or in the Galley. Similarly, leak stopping

---

* A bin bag (in which a discarded cigarette might cause a fire).

might be required if the ship has collided with another vessel or the jetty, or if an area of internal high pressure salt water main piping has ruptured.

Mercifully, the chances of serving in a chemical, biological or radioactive warfare environment are rare but nonetheless these eventualities are covered. Submariners will very rarely need such training, and although they are issued with personal respirators, these are rarely, if ever, taken out of their haversacks for the rest of their careers.

Personnel are issued with respirators during their initial training, and although not specifically tailored to the size and features on one's head, they generally come in three sizes. The respirators are supposed to be designed to enable personnel to communicate, eat and drink. In reality, it is impossible to understand what another person is saying, and if one were to place one's head underwater and listen to someone talking outside of the water, one would gain an understanding of the actual standard of conversation. Hand signals are more appropriate.

If a ship is suspected of entering a chemical, biological or radioactive environment it may undertake a 'prewet' evolution. At this point, the ship charges its internal high-pressure salt water system and discharges the water onto the upper deck using small outlets. This creates a dome of water which both protects the upper deck from chemical droplets, and will be used in conjunction with forced roll, in other words when the ship deliberately disengages its stabilizers and exacerbates rudder movements to aid the removal of substances from the upper deck. If any personnel are employed on the upper deck and are at greater risk of exposure to the effects of CBRN warfare, they will be required to re-enter the ship by only one entry point (known as the cleansing station). When doing so, they will be stripped of their suspected contaminated clothing in a sterile compartment. Unfortunately, many ships elect to stow their gash in cleansing stations while deployed, thereby not making it sterile nor especially clean.

From time to time, personnel are required to verify that their respirator is indeed airtight. This is achieved by wearing the respirator and entering a compartment ashore into which harmless gas pellets are placed, in which the wearer is required to demonstrate the ability to change a filter canister in a gas-filled environment. Alternatively, a portable capability is carried in ships, which comprises an airtight small tent in which an individual will sit. Their respirator is attached to a laptop, and the wearer will have to shake their head from side to side, nod up and down and simulate chewing in order to determine whether the airtight seal is maintained. Sometimes personnel are asked to undertake all three movements at the same time.

'D'you hear there, the Ship's Office will be open for the next 1 minute for cheque cashing and exchange of giblets.'

This pipe indicates that the Ship's Office is opening for a short period of time to enable the ship's company to cash a cheque. It also means that the ship will shortly visit Gibraltar (Gib). For those sailors who have never been to Gibraltar, the ship's PO Writer, in a rare display of humour, will invite naive young sailors to exchange sterling for the local currency, giblets*.

Playing pranks on unseasoned sailors or visitors can be amusing. As we now know, it is not uncommon for visitors to be presented with a bill for the electricity used while their bunk light was lit. Sailors on their first visit to Scotland might be invited to attend a haggis shoot.

Gibraltar is a run ashore of which legends are made. Despite the contribution to the local economy, many years ago sailors might not have been particularly liked by the local constabulary. During my second visit there in HMS *Nottingham*, four sailors were returned by the police in two hours. The morning watch as the Second Officer of the Day flew by.

Runs ashore in Gib follow a fixed routine. Arrive, go ashore, get leathered, return onboard at 0400. Two hours later many members of the ship's company gather to commence the Rock Race. The roads of Gib are temporarily closed for this evolution. While some believe this is to avoid a road traffic accident it is more likely to protect the locals from viewing the delivery of dockyard pizzas (i.e. people vomiting).

---

* This is not a recognized currency.

Arriving at Gib tends to mean that the deployment has really started and while there is a natural sense of sadness at having left families behind for six to nine months, there is also the anticipation of the adventures ahead.

At the end of a run ashore the following may be piped: **'D'you hear there, reverse cheque cashing will take place in the Ship's Office for the next one zero* minutes.'**

The Ship's Office is a small compartment in the ship inhabited by Writers. The personnel in this office deal with correspondence, pay and cash (sterling, and, when abroad, foreign exchange cashing). The senior member of the Ship's Office team is either a PO or CPO Writer. Although they are there to provide a service similar to a bank, the PO Writer opens at a time of their choosing and does not always provide a cheerful service.

On this occasion the PO Writer has afforded 10 minutes of their day, to perform a basic function for the ship's company. Although it is now easier to pay for souvenirs (known as 'gizzits'), or services using a bank card or phone when abroad, the RN does provide a foreign exchange service for personnel often at very preferential rates (and without commission). Many years ago, the currency would have initially been provided by writing a cheque. Before each port visit each person would have carefully studied their finances to see how much money they had, and how much they might wish to spend on their run ashore. A failure to accurately predict either of those factors would lead to a bounced cheque or a visit to a cash point. Alternatively, if the cheque took a significant amount of time to return to the UK and be cleared through the UK banking system, it might make it difficult for a sailor to keep abreast of their finances. In modern times, such activity is enabled by sophisticated IT, but there was at least one occasion when a sailor proceeding on draft from a ship (i.e. when they left the ship for the final time before moving to another ship) was tasked to take an envelope of cheques back to

---

* 'One zero' minutes = 10 minutes. I do not know why the word 'ten' is not used.

the UK to enable swifter processing. It is my understanding that the envelope was deposited in a bin at the airport.

The distribution of currency would have usually been conducted by mess. Each mess would choose a person (usually the junior person) to be their focal point for foreign currency cashing, and their job would have been to collect firstly the cheques from their mess mates, and then the corresponding (probably very considerable) amount of money on behalf of those mess mates, and then distribute it. Lots could go wrong.

The currency itself would be embarked prior to sailing from UK, usually in US dollars and the currency of the first planned port visit. Thereafter, other currencies would be embarked by the embassy representative or the ship's agent as required. They would do this by placing the currency in a bag, with a quoit and line attached in case it dropped in the water and sank while being carried over the Gangway. The PO Writer and LO would count the cash and wash their hands eight times after doing so.

Armed with their money, sailors would proceed ashore. The Navy would compensate sailors for the higher prices usually associated with a run ashore by providing an allowance specific to the certain location; however, the allowance (known as Local Overseas Allowance or LOA) would, for some unfathomable reason, vary depending on one's rank. Prior to arrival in a port, the ship would be told the different rates for different ranks/rates. There was seemingly no real logic to why a Commander would receive the top rate of LOA, as would a leading hand, whereas a PO could receive the same rate as a sub-lieutenant. Apparently it was to do with the type of thing a different rank (or demographic) might typically purchase whereas, in actual fact, they were all likely to purchase the same items, namely beer, food, postcards, haircuts and woodies (wood carvings) in Africa.

The basis of the LOA calculation would be a mythical shopping basket of items which one might typically wish to purchase. The Navy actually paid three LOs based in London to fly around the world from time to time to update the price of the basket. Tough job.

Anyone with ickies left over from the run ashore would be able to convert their currency back into sterling in order for it to be used in the ship's micro economy which revolved around the CANMAN, or dhobeymen. This was known as reverse cheque cashing, and the pipe was an indicator that the run ashore was coming to an end. It was unlikely that many people would have much currency left over unless they had been put 'on puns'* (having been the subject of a 'report to the Regulating Office' pipe) or become injured as a result of overindulgence on 'the first night in' (which actually means 'out'!).

There are certain things that will almost certainly happen during a port visit: a cocktail party (see page 116), a Captain's lunch party (attended by the mayor, attaché and officer under training), a party for local children, a Ship Open to Visitors (SOTV), an invitation onboard from the POs to nurses, a fight ashore and sports fixtures between local teams. If another RN warship is alongside, and it is from a different base port, a fight will probably take place between members of each ship, whereas the Wardroom will have a 'call around'. It is likely that the junior captain will also have to pay a visit to the senior captain.

A party for local schoolchildren (particularly underprivileged children) will invariably tug at the benevolent nature of most sailors, and there will usually be an abundance of volunteers to help organize the party. On a similar note, opportunities for personnel to visit and help maintain local orphanages are usually oversubscribed. There are considerably fewer volunteers to help organize SOTV. During SOTV, the helicopter is usually placed on the flight deck and the hangar will contain very dull noticeboards showing photographs of the roles of each department. The Captain's lunch party is likely to be a discreet affair, although for a visit to a ship's affiliated town or city a much larger dinner might take place for all affiliates in the Wardroom. The chefs provide a very high level of food for these occasions – although I was once disappointed that butterscotch Angel Delight was provided for a senior officer. On another occasion, diners were saddened to see the mayor of a British town lick his plate.

A Visit Liaison Team will be appointed to organize and coordinate each port visit. This will usually be formed of a junior officer (lieutenant or sub-lieutenant), a senior rating, an officer under

---

* Under punishment, with stoppage of leave.

training and a CW candidate[*]. The job of these team members is to consult the Port Guide and liaise with organizations in the port to provide opportunities for entertainment and recreation. They are quite similar to very amateur travel agents or resort reps. As part of the information they impart to the ship's company, the team will inform personnel of the recommended places to visit as well as the locations ashore which are deemed out of bounds. The out-of-bounds locations are likely to be frequented by members of the ship's company.

'D'you hear there, the last PAS boat will depart in 10 minutes time.'

Occasionally, visits to distant and exotic places are undertaken with the ship at anchor or at a buoy due to the lack of available or suitable berths. This places a number of limitations on the ship's company. Firstly, there is no Gangway from the ship to the shore, which means that proceeding ashore and returning onboard are wholly reliant on a PAS boat (i.e. a small passenger vessel) operated by a local boat driver, who is presumably now living in retirement having fleeced HM Government for the provision of this service. Secondly, the ship will only allow 50 per cent leave at any one time, ensuring that there is a suitable number of personnel onboard to deal with emergencies or take the ship to sea in the event of very inclement weather.

The realization that the final opportunity to step ashore is approaching renders panic in all those who said they were being good and would actually not go ashore, but who, since their oppos went ashore three hours previously, have been drinking onboard and now regret their decision. They therefore make an on-the-spot decision to make that final PAS boat, and in that 10 minutes can

---

[*] CW candidates are ratings who are deemed to be 'commission worthy'. In a bid to demonstrate their worthiness for promotion to the upper deck and to become officers, CW candidates are obvious attendees at a cocktail party (CTP).

achieve a dhobey (shower), put their civvies/ironed denim jeans on, phone the QM and say, 'Hold the PAS boat, we're on our way,' and have another round of rum – and the senior rates appear on the upper deck ready to go! In their rush they will ask the QM to 'peg us out please, shipmate'. The QM may ask them to bring back some 'big eats'.

A record of who is onboard is kept by a rudimentary pegging in and out board. This is typically a multi-faced rotating cylinder with each face representing a messdeck. There is a hole and a peg for each person in that mess, and the peg is placed in 'Onboard' or 'Ashore' or 'On Leave' depending on one's location. Hence, 'Peg us in please, shipwreck!'* The Wardroom will have a crafted wooden board with each officer's name, and instead of a peg they will have a slide to indicate whether they are onboard or ashore.

---

* Sailors often use a variety of different words derived from 'shipmate', such as shipwreck, shippers, shipshape. For example, if someone asks for a sip of your drink they might say 'sippers shippers'.

Returning onboard, via a PAS boat, accommodation ladder or gangway, can be a challenge if one has taken in drink. A heavy dose of booze might require a period of time and reflection at the bottom of the Gangway while one composes oneself. This results in a steady, laborious inch-by-inch slow-motion clamber up the Gangway (dislodging a lightbulb while in transit) and, for an officer, an attempt to stand to attention on a metal block of two steps. Depending on the state of the tide and the length of one's legs, the drop from the Gangway to the metal steps on the flight deck can be perilous irrespective of whether in drink or not. Having noted that the officer has stood to attention, the Gangway staff might wearily return this with a 'butt' salute of the rifle and a helpful 'Don't worry, Sir/Ma'am, I'll peg you in'.

Officers salute at the top of the Gangway as a traditional mark of respect to the quarterdeck, which had a religious significance in years gone by. Although the Gangway is now usually located away from the quarterdeck, the tradition is maintained, and is now observed by all members of the ship's company.

I was fortunate to have several anchor/buoy runs ashore including Istanbul (twice), Akrotiri (for a month), Tristan da Cunha, Port San Carlos, Port Stanley, Mahe (Seychelles), Rothesay and Salcombe.

Strictly speaking, Port San Carlos was not a run ashore. It was an opportunity to proceed ashore and pay respects to the sailors, Marines, soldiers and airmen who lost their lives in this area of the Falkland Islands in 1982. It is a vivid memory and a privilege to have stood in the cemetery with my ship in the background close to the spot where so many ships and sailors fought gallantly.

On that same deployment we had a run ashore at anchor to Tristan da Cunha, an isolated island in the South Atlantic. It was not particularly memorable. We took an RAF man with us whose job was to blow up some volcanic rock which was blocking the harbour. I do not think it was successful. I also recall the island having a few hundred occupants and only a few surnames ...

Day 49

Peg Me Out Shipmate!

LOCATION: AT SEA/RIO DE JANEIRO

'Out all gash, out all gash … all personnel not on watch, muster on the Gangway.'

After several weeks at sea the ship has the chance to remove its gash. The 'Gash PO' or Clubz might take charge of this evolution. Up until that point the gash may have either been stored on the quarterdeck (next to the tabbers) or in the inappropriately named 'cleansing station', which will now need to be cleaned. It is likely that those individuals who were required to report to the Regulating Office at various times will be required to clean the cleansing station so that it can be put to its proper use.

This evolution presents a moral dilemma to some officers, who grapple with the issue of believing that they do not have to handle the gash because they have earned the privilege of drinking moose's milk* in the Wardroom instead, while others give in to their moral conscience that directs that they too created the waste so it is only right that they help remove it. This one goes to the very heart of Royal Naval social structure. Those officers who do take part in the removal of gash will wear sparkling white, stiff, overalls.

This issue occasionally causes arguments in the Wardroom when those who have helped with the gash (usually loggies, engineers and the Bish) return to find other members of the Wardroom (Bridge watchkeepers) becoming merrily inebriated. The arguments tend to subside once a '70s, '80s, Elvis or Neil Diamond CD is played

---

* Moose's milk is a potent ice cream-based cocktail originating from Canada.

(and once the Deputy Weapon Engineering Officer (DWEO)[*] has unravelled the snakes' wedding of audio cables), and when 'chips at six' arrive. It is not known whether such social divisions occurred in the chiefs' mess or indeed if they turn to for this evolution.

Devonport-based sailors will often refer to a Portsmouth ship as a 'Pompey gashbarge', and they often use an even less pleasant word for Portsmouth itself.

In Devonport, it is not unusual to have a Portsmouth-based ship berth alongside the Devonport-based ship (for example, when undertaking OST). In such circumstances, one might hear the pipe: **'D'you hear there, the Pompey gashbarge is now alongside, port side to.'**

This will raise a titter or scowl.

'PO Caterer, visitor, jetty.'
This means that provisions have arrived on the jetty and, unless they are purely milk and bread, they will require a major 'store ship' to be undertaken.

In such circumstances the following pipe will be made shortly afterwards: **'D'you hear there, clear lower deck of all personnel not on watch, muster on the flight deck.'**

This pipe should come as no surprise as the likelihood of a major 'store ship' will have been detailed on Daily Orders (... which everyone reads ...). As with 'Out All Gash', it is unlikely that all officers will attend this evolution.

There are a number of aspects to a major 'store ship', which are as follows:

1. Provisions arrive by lorry and/or refrigerated truck on the jetty at midday in baking hot heat. The provisions will have been sourced by the ship's agent. The agent will typically

---

[*] An officer who, by virtue of nothing other than an A Level in Physics, is adjudged to be a techno-wizard.

thank the LO, Captain and PO Caterer by showing some hospitality ashore; either a meal or ... other stuff. A number of expenses are incurred by a ship during a port visit, ranging from food, tugs and fenders (whether you want them or not – very expensive) to the pilot, removal of waste fluids, removal of gash and taxi drivers returning drunk sailors (not a Crown expense). Ships have occasionally been known to pay for items which have subsequently been considered inadmissible as a Crown expense – such as a video projector.

2. The PO Caterer is assumed to be the inspector of fine produce and will therefore handle and smell the fresh produce in order to confirm quality.

3. The LO (unless they are an SD/SUY Caterer) will know very little about the quality of the food (nor indeed will they know anything about stores (toilet rolls), cash or pay,[*] or anything to do with logistics for that matter). The LO will, however, be very bright; they will be renowned for having scored higher than any other officer at their AIB, thereby earning the right to have 'all night in' (i.e. not have to undertake any watches). The role of the LO during a store ship is to physically count all the provisions – although they don't really, especially the meat, unless they personally weigh it (by which time it has thawed).

4. The ship's company will form a human chain from the truck, along the jetty, up the Gangway, along the upper deck (i.e. 1 Deck), into the ship, down to 2 Deck, and probably to 3 Deck, where the food will be stowed by one of the leading hand chefs in the Fridge (cool room) or Freezer (cold room) (if they are serviceable) or the Dry Store. It is not unusual for Fridges or Freezers to be defective, and *in extremis* a temporary (but semi-permanent) chillcon will be placed on the flight deck. There are three issues of note with the presence of a chillcon: it can cause stability issues for the ship, it is yet another example of the versatility of a flight deck and it will require duty personnel to frequently inspect the chillcon to ensure that it

---

[*] Unless an SD/SUY Jack Dusty or Writer.

has not become defective. If the chillcon breaks and all of the stored food perishes, the ship might have to use its emergency provisions; these are otherwise known as tinned ravioli and have a shelf life of 40 years (the lifespan of a Type 23 frigate).
5. Once the stores party is mustered, the food will be passed or thrown along the human chain. Choc ices will be transported onto the ship by an armed guard.

Once the provisions are safely onboard and stowed, the ship will be able to determine its endurance (i.e. how long can it stay at sea). This endurance calculation is highly complicated and is based on the following:

1. How much meat do we have? Unless one is in a carrier, where this is amended to tomahawk steaks.
2. How much pasta, potatoes and rice do we have?
3. How many vegetables do we have?
4. Whichever of the above is the smallest quantity will primarily determine the ship's endurance. However, the added complication of portion control will ultimately decide this. Two options are available: either let people eat as much as they wish or exercise strict portion control (as practised by every submarine).

The LO will report the ship's logistics state to the Captain once per week. The Captain is unlikely ask any questions, thereby saving the LO any embarrassment.

Food, of course, is a vital element of life onboard a warship, and serves the following functions:

1. It provides nourishment.
2. It provides the senior rates with something to moan about, unless of course the PO Caterer is providing them with cheese. Cheese, incidentally, is a scarce commodity onboard a warship. Officers have to pay an extra charge on their mess bill for cheese (or tartare sauce). This is known as Extra Messing Charge (EMC). In theory senior ratings also have to pay such a charge for cheese. From my time at sea I am unsure whether

they actually ever did pay or just thought it was free (i.e. like batteries), or whether the officers unknowingly paid for it.
3. It enables sailors to know what day it is without using a calendar. Friday is likely to be curry night. Saturday is steak or chicken Kiev night. Sunday is roast. In serious terms, adding variety to a menu is a welcome addition to life onboard particularly during a long ocean transit or a period on patrol in Defence Watches. It is all the more remarkable given that the chefs have a budget of approximately 47 pence per sailor per day (which, it was claimed, was less than that of a prison's catering budget). Occasionally, the ship may have a pizza night sponsored by one of the messdecks. On such occasions, non-chefs are allowed into the Galley to help prepare pizzas. Personnel are able to phone the Galley from their messdeck and order pizzas and, if properly considered before the ship deploys, some actual pizza boxes will be available. Telephoning the Galley is not always to be recommended as it is likely that the chef's response and manner will be an abrupt 'What do you want?', but the novelty of being in the Galley will make other sailors temporarily happy, although it will ultimately confirm to them why they chose not to be a chef.

Although the pizza night provisions will be paid at Crown expense, a nominal charge will be made for the pizza (unless an HM Treasury official has decreed that this is inappropriate), and those funds either will go directly into the ship's welfare fund or will be given to one of the ship's nominated charities. There are, of course, thousands of needy charities in the UK, and it is not unusual for units to nominate a charity local to their affiliated town (such as a home for stray cats). I never quite understood why units did not put their charitable proceeds to the Royal Naval Association (which may look after them once sailors become veterans) or other Service charities; however, the links with affiliated towns are strong and highly valued by both the ships and the towns themselves. Some ships have been, or still are, affiliated to towns which promised fabulous runs ashore (e.g. Glasgow, Cardiff, Newcastle, London, Edinburgh, Liverpool, Manchester and Nottingham). In Somerset we had Avonmouth.

A variety of charitable endeavours will usually be undertaken by sailors during long deployments reflecting, by their nature, the generosity of sailors towards those less well off than themselves. Such endeavours include running around the upper deck (without being hit by an opening door), rowing the equivalent of the miles steamed by the ship on deployment, village fetes and running up the Rock (of Gibraltar) (see page 101).

'Attention on the upper deck, face to starboard, Vice Admiral Sir Lee Kennington DSO CB CBE KCB, Second Sea Lord and Deputy Chief of the Naval Staff.'
This pipe is alerting the ship's company that an admiral, in this case the Second Sea Lord, is due to arrive onboard for a preplanned visit. It is important that the full title of the Admiral is included in addition to all post-nominals, in the correct order (unlike this occasion). The Admiral will arrive in a car with a flag on the front and full beam headlights, and any passing sailor must stop and salute as the car passes through the dockyard. Sometimes the Admiral will arrive by taxi (i.e. the ship's helicopter), and will have sat on an inflatable chair during the journey.

The arrival of an admiral matters little to most members of the ship's company except, perhaps, the Captain, who might consider this to be quality face time that might aid subsequent promotion. For this reason it is likely to matter to the First Lieutenant and the heads of department as well.

For most of the rest of the ship's company it is likely to mean significant time cleaning the ship. They will know that the only person who really cares about this visit is the Big Dipper (skipper). Skippers of ships do not like being referred to as 'skippers'. They tend to say that 'only fishing boats have skippers'. Nonetheless, most of the ship's company will still refer to the skipper as 'the Skipper'.

The Admiral is likely to undertake fireside chats with the various messes during which the sailors will be updated on the state of the Navy, and why they have the best pension in the public sector despite the sailor not getting a penny if they leave after 19 years.

There is, of course, no fireside beside which to chat. Instead, the Admiral will sit in a comfy chair and the other attendees will sit in a circle. The Admiral will probably be provided with a plate of biscuits which they are unlikely eat. Those biscuits might be free 'NAAFI' biscuits or the mess may dig into their own pockets to buy chocolate biscuits. It is also highly likely that the Admiral will be provided with a cup of tea with a saucer (even in the stokers' mess) although, to highlight their authentic roots, they might insist on using a mug. During the course of the conversation, when boredom might quickly set in, the sailors' eyes might stray to the colour of the Admiral's socks, which may not be in keeping with uniform regulations. This will annoy some people. Maybe they just faded in the laundry. However, I did once spy that an admiral had a motif of 'Bully' from *Bullseye* on his black (dark grey) socks.

The sailors are likely to raise topics which have changed little over time. The topics entail the ship's programme, pay (including Pay 2000 when that was introduced [*]), medals, allowances and pay (again).

Prior to arriving onboard, the Admiral is likely to have been provided with a brief on the ship, its programme and its key personnel. The brief itself will have been largely written by the ship's officers, and it will have had at least 15 iterations. Despite the time writing and rewriting the brief, it will still contain several errors by the time the Admiral reads it (if indeed they do read it). The brief should contain the names of any members of the ship's company who have worked with the Admiral before, and therefore help the Admiral remember their names when they meet.

During the visit, the Admiral may be invited to present medals to members of the ship's company. It is not unusual for sailors *not*

---

[*] Pay 2000 was a highly emotive change to sailors' pay which moved pay from being the same for all irrespective of their branch to a system whereby different branches were assessed and graded, and paid on a high or low pay band. Many felt that this shifted away from a sense of 'all of one company'. Very few people thought it was a good idea, even those who tried to justify it at fireside chats.

to want the Admiral to present the medal. Many prefer the more dignified process of having the medal presented by a Writer in the Ship's Office, and be asked to sign for it.

Towards the end of the visit, the ship's company might be required to attend a 'clear lower deck' with the Admiral. The Admiral may give a speech which will have been drafted by their Secretary or Flag Lieutenant. It might include a joke which is marginally funny, but nonetheless, people will politely laugh.

Having left the ship, the Admiral will have a much better understanding of the Captain and whether they merit promotion. If the Captain has impressed, the Admiral they may be subsequently adjudged as follows ... 'Lieutenant Commander Davey is the best small ship commanding officer in the surface flotilla' in their annual appraisal report. If, on the other hand, the Captain is considered to be ranked Number 10 of 10 candidates, they will not be described as '10 of 10' (i.e. the worst), but instead will be described as 'in the top ten COs in the surface flotilla'. This is aimed at masking the fact that the CO has not featured strongly, and will try to stop them from leaving the Navy by suggesting that they feature somewhere high in the top 10. In other words, 'damning with faint praise'.

In days gone by, the annual appraisal report was known as an S206. Thus, before the visit of the Admiral, the Captain might have informed the officers that 'there are 206 reasons to get this right'.

Incidentally, during the Admiral's visit it is likely that the QM/BM or HQ1 watchkeeper will have been told to keep routine pipes to an absolute minimum so as not to irritate the Admiral or the Captain. Unfortunately, this will soon be forgotten and it is possible that the First Lieutenant will become angry on hearing the pipe **'Writer Complin, Regulating Office'** while in the Wardroom fireside chat. The First Lieutenant may become so angry that they will get up and phone the Bridge and whisper (loudly), 'What part of no routine pipes do you not understand?' Despite the lack of routine pipes, it is amazing how much of the ship's routine will continue unhindered.

Very few people will be sad to see the Admiral leave.

'D'you hear there, Free Gangway will close at 1755, and will reopen at 2200.'

This pipe will provide different thoughts depending on one's role in a ship. The pipe will almost certainly mean, on the first day alongside abroad, that there is going to be a cocktail party (CTP). Given that the guests will board the ship via the Gangway, it is preferred that sailors, in whatever state of dress they have chosen, should not be leaving the ship, or returning onboard, while the CTP is underway. Thus, the Gangway is closed for this period, and the only people who can board or depart are the guests. So, for most sailors, it means that if they want to get ashore they need to have a dhobey, get changed into their civvies, and be off the ship by 1755. They will need to entertain themselves ashore until at least 2200. Those who have not gone ashore are duty, or have volunteered to help with the CTP, or are stewards, or are under puns. CW candidates are likely to be in attendance. The officers and very senior ratings (i.e. warrant officers) are required onboard.

A CTP will take place either in the hangar or on the flight deck, depending on the ship's location and climate, and most of the afternoon will have been spent rigging an awning (marquee) on the flight deck, floodlights to make the ship look pretty (or a target) or nice bunting, such as flags or ensigns, in the hangar. The officers under training (OUTs)/young officers (YOs) and sub-lieutenants (SLUTs/Snotties) will have been directed to construct a rockery (with a waterfall).

Prior to the event commencing, a number of things will have happened. Some of the officers will have gathered in the Wardroom for a sharpener. The Warfare Officers, in celebration of having done their job and in the knowledge that it ceases once alongside, will have been 'on it' for a number of hours and will gradually be joined by their other colleagues who, as we now know, will have been turned to during the day to help ditch gash and store ship. They will eventually change into their smarter uniform for the CTP (No. 1 uniform or tropical white uniform with open-necked bush jacket), and will be briefed by the First Lieutenant. Some of the officers will take the role of being a hooker (not a prostitute) for the evening. In general, personnel perform the following roles:

PEG ME OUT SHIPMATE!

CO and XO: head meeters and greeters at the Gangway, armed with a telescope.

Gangway staff: piping the side for every foreign officer, and helping ladies in high heels onto the flight deck. They do not peg anyone in or out.

Heads of department and senior lieutenants: they will gather in small circular groups ready to receive guests from the hookers.

Junior officers (aka hookers): their role is to 'hook' each guest and escort them to the small circular groups. Occasionally, if the guests have been spotted making their way along the Gangway, a hooker might be taken aside by one of the groups and be asked (gently ordered) either to bring particular guests to them, or to ensure they go to another group.

A range of drinks will be offered: horse's neck, gin and tonic, maybe beer,* soft drinks and wine. Wine will usually be poured from bottles. (On one occasion one unnamed CO did not approve of my using cheaper wine from boxes, but was pleased when the PO Steward informed him that it was being decanted into bottles to create a sophisticated illusion while saving the Crown some money.) All of the food and drink needs to be appropriately accounted and recorded.

The chefs will have been busy either preparing 'smally eats' or defrosting them. It is likely that during the same working day they will have prepared breakfast, lunch and dinner for the ship's company, as well as cook a three-course fine dining lunch for the CO and guests. The stewards will be preparing the drinks and presentational touches (which are, literally, without fault). They might be assisted by other sailors. All sailors supporting the CTP are likely to enjoy any surplus beverages during or after the event, and will usually be seen doing so in the Wardroom pantry. I still have cocktail sticks in the pockets of some pieces of uniform.

The CTP guests are likely to have been invited by the British Embassy, High Commission or RN Liaison Officer. They will typically be dignitaries, local politicians, wealthy expats, golf club secretaries,

---

* Though not in HMS *Somerset* (1998/99) or HMS *Chatham* (2003/04).

nurses (it is true, in days gone by) and foreign military officers. Each foreign military officer will be entitled to a salute at the top of the Gangway. Their salutes will range from a Kenny Everett-style US salute to a slow languid turn to the White Ensign. The rest of the evening will be spent trying to find something interesting to talk about, ideally in English.

As mentioned in an earlier pipe, I do not know how five ladies of the night found their way into a CTP in Rio. It appeared that although a guest list was available at the Gangway, the five ladies chanced their arms some time after most of the guests had been greeted by the CO. The officer under training who was placed at the top of the Gangway to greet any stragglers appears to have panicked or been overcome at their arrival, and ushered them to the bar. The hooker brought the lady to my circle whereupon I innocently enquired, 'What do you do?' Unfortunately, I do not speak Portuguese and neither did most of them speak English. Nonetheless, the senior, older lady informed me that she was an 'entertainer and escort'. By that time, my cabin mate had already invited them back to the Wardroom for post-CTP drinks. Having decided that they were ladies of the night, we concluded that they should probably not stay for the party, and we politely withdrew their invitation. Also, slightly later in the evening, the Wardroom members, in their finest rig, valiantly formed a fire party (not to be confused with the Wardroom Party) to help fight a fire onboard RFA *Grey Rover* (which was berthed astern of us).

The evening will draw to a close with the ceremony of Sunset or Evening Colours. This is, as we know from page 15, when the White Ensign is lowered, and the King is put to bed. It is an important occasion under any circumstance, but a ceremonial Sunset or Evening Colours does, for both guest and serviceperson, instil a moment of pride and reflection that this is a piece of the United Kingdom abroad. The duty watch will undertake this ceremony under significantly more pressure than normal. The Rating responsible for the Union Jack will have dipped in, because nobody of note will see them perform the relatively easy task of lowering the Union Flag. Some officers might find that they still have their glass in their hand at the critical moment of the White Ensign being lowered, and will quietly try and hide their glass or will try to work out whether they should be stood at ease or at attention. They hope no-one will see them gently try to assume the correct posture.

If the occasion is particularly significant, Evening Colours or Sunset will be accompanied by the Band of His Majesty's Royal Marines.

During the ceremony, the stewards will have quietly closed the bar, and this should be the cue for guests to leave the ship. Sometimes this cue is not taken, and it might take some time to ask people to leave, ensuring that the same saluting process takes place as they depart. Fortunately, the Captain or First Lieutenant will still have their telescope under their left arm to spot any Spanish or French ships of the line.

Once the CTP is complete, the officers will retire to the Wardroom. This is likely to lead to a party into the early hours of the following morning.

I have had some memorable and enjoyable CTPs: Rio, Belfast, Palma, Seychelles, Freetown, Port Stanley and Cape Town. Cape Verde (before it was popular) was dull because the ship sailed immediately after the CTP finished; indeed SSDCUADCS3CY (see page 40) was piped prior to Evening Colours. During that visit we did, however, beat the local cricket team (whose average age was 70). As I possessed a blazer, I was directed to assume the role of Captain.

A variation of this pipe is as follows: **'D'you hear there, Free Gangway is closed until further notice!'**

This means that nobody (I repeat, nobody) is allowed to proceed ashore under any circumstances. The pipe is likely to lead to the subsequent pipe, made by either the First Lieutenant or the EWO, informing the ship's company that one of the Navy's Compulsory Drug Teams (CDT) is onboard, and will test some of, or all, members of the ship's company for the use of banned substances. Only a very small number of personnel onboard (probably the Captain and First Lieutenant) will be aware of the arrival of the CDT in advance. The CDT can also be requested by the Captain. In days gone by, when banned substances were less prevalent on UK streets, the CDT could probably be guaranteed after a ship's visit to Amsterdam.

During the visit of the CDT a list will be created of all personnel onboard, and only those who are not selected for testing, or who have been tested, are allowed ashore. The test will be provided by way of a urine sample, and the donor of the sample has to be observed providing the sample (but protecting some privacy and dignity).

Anyone testing positive for a banned substance will, in all but very exceptional circumstances, be discharged from the Royal Navy.

'D'you hear there, leave, leave in accordance with daily orders!'

This is usually a time of happiness which signifies the end of the working day. Typically, if one was to place oneself in any of the airlocks (i.e. exit points onto the upper deck) within 5 minutes of the pipe, one would find most of the WE senior rates already in their civvies ready to step foot on to the Gangway immediately. Most will have also asked the QM to 'peg me out' in order to win an extra 5 seconds leave.

Some of the previous pipes have provided an insight into the various states of dress and activity prior to proceeding on leave.

This pipe will have subtly different consequences and aspects depending on whether the ship is in its base port or whether it is deployed.

If the ship is in its base port, sailors may proceed ashore for their journey home and will join a queue of cars from the dockyard resembling Moses' exodus from Egypt. Alternatively, they may proceed into Portsmouth, Guzz or Helensburgh (or Rosyth a very long time ago) for a run ashore. If proceeding on leave for a prolonged period, for example over Christmas, they will eventually return mulling over what their computer password or safe combination is, or indeed contemplating submitting their notice[*].

---

[*] Otherwise known as 'banging out', 'putting my chit in' or 'seven clicks to freedom' (signifying the seven clicks of a mouse along the steps to submitting notice on the Joint Personnel Administration system).

If leaving the ship in order to proceed on draft, the sailor will be armed with all of their belongings, gizzits (i.e. memorabilia from their time onboard) and leaving gifts.

If the ship has just returned from a deployment before proceeding on leave, this will be an especially happy time. It is likely that the ship will have spent the previous night at anchor off Portsmouth or Devonport where, although they are not allowed to have an 'up Channel night", there probably will have been some form of unofficial celebration in each messdeck, which may subsequently lead to a pipe for someone to report to the Regulating Office. The following morning, before proceeding from anchor to the reunion with families and friends at the jetty, the ship might be lucky or unlucky to have a visit from an admiral who will tell them that 'they have done very well'. The ship's company will be keen to see the admiral leave. The senior rates are likely to have pre-arranged bunches of roses for their partners, and if it is a Guzz ship, it may have arranged for a boat transfer of 'oggies' (pasties). All of the ship's company will dress in their No. 1 uniform ready to greet their families.

If deployed, the period of leave is likely to be night leave only, usually expiring at approximately 0700 the following day. Occasionally, station leave may be granted to allow for a prolonged period of time away from the ship.

The piping of leave is generally welcomed; however, the piping of **'Leave by department'** is generally not welcomed, especially when deployed, as it tends to mean the stokers and loggies will still be turned to for several hours while other members of the ship's company merrily proceed ashore. Some members of the ship's company may have never heard the pipe for 'Leave', given that they are already ashore (WEs and WAFUs).

If the ship is imminently proceeding to sea, the 'Leave' pipe will be accompanied by the following pipe: **'The ship's company is reminded that the ship is under sailing orders!'**

---

* Final night at sea party.

This addendum is essentially a reminder to the ship's company that under the circumstances of the ship imminently sailing, were they to be adrift, they would risk returning to the jetty to find that the ship has sailed! It also means that if they do return to the ship adrift when it is under sailing orders, not only will they be piped to the Regulating Office, but their punishment fine is likely to be much greater than in other circumstances.

Ghost Pipes

All of the pipes detailed in the book were, and to a large degree still are, broadcast over ships' main broadcast equipment. However, it will probably have been noted that there are times at sea when life can become dull. Sailors are humorous but, on occasion, they can let their humour get the better of them, and even if not warranting a pipe to 'report to the Regulating Office', this might involve a conversation with the First Lieutenant.

There have been occasions where a sailor (usually the BM, but it might be someone who happened to use the main broadcast without authority) would make a pipe in order to gain a titter from the rest of the ship's company.

Such pipes are as follows:

'D'you hear there, Mr Liam Gallagher, OASIS Maintainer, contact the SCC.'

Quite often when alongside, ships will be visited by civilian contractors to maintain or fix items of equipment which are beyond the expertise of the ship's company. RN ships used to use an application known as OASIS for the use of stores accounting, engineering planning and word processing. The SCC is, of course, the Ship's Control Centre. On this occasion, the ghost piper has combined the name of the Gallagher pop duo with the OASIS system. Some people onboard (i.e. quite old CPOs, three-badge ABs and the CANMAN) will have had no idea that this was a joke.

'D'you hear there, Leading Seaman Krankee, Small Arms Store.'

Many younger readers will be unfamiliar with the Krankee comedy husband/wife duo. The wife (whose real name was Janette Tough) was especially small, enabling her to portray the character of a very small boy (i.e. with small arms). The Small Arms Store is where pistols are stowed. Hence, Leading Seaman Krankee, Small Arms Store.

'D'you hear there, leave! … leave your civvies in your locker, there is no leave.'
A derivation of the 'Leave' pipe in which sailors are effectively told to leave your uniform on and keep working … there is no leave!

'Officer of the Watch, Bridge.'
This pipe is not necessarily humorous, but it is very unusual and slightly alarming. When at sea, the OOW should be on the Bridge at all times; nowhere else. Hence, if one hears this pipe, it indicates that the OOW is either incapacitated, dead or, more likely, in an extreme amount of trouble, or that it is a joke.

OR

'Quartermaster, Gangway.'
This is similar to the previous pipe as, when alongside, the QM should be at the Gangway at all times. However, such a pipe may happen when a BM is undertaking their first ever Gangway watch and the QM disappears for a quick trip to the heads. This, technically, is not allowed as both the QM and BM always need to be at the Gangway. However, an innocent new BM might not think of the consequences of piping the QM to the Gangway. It is likely to make the rest of the watch quite painful.

'D'you hear there, the person borrowing tennis equipment from the PT store is to return the rackets to the same, and balls to the Master at Arms.'
Clubz will carry a range of sports equipment onboard for use either at sea or when alongside, and it is not unusual for such equipment to be borrowed but not returned in a timely manner. This pipe is asking that whoever borrowed the equipment should return the tennis rackets to the PT store, and [the] balls to the MAA. To many, this pipe might not raise an eyebrow until they realize that there is no need to return any balls to the MAA and, in fact, they are saying 'balls to the MAA!' in an entirely different context.

'D'you hear there, no smoking, no naked lights on the starboard waist, milac spillage.'
A derivation of the (very serious) pipe on page 58, but this refers to the much less (zero) risk associated with the spillage of milac[*]!

---

[*] Long-life milk.

'Meeeooww.'
Someone attempting to be the ship's cat.
'D'you hear there, the person holding the Buffer's ten-ton test tackles, report to the Buffer's store.'
This is likely to be a pipe made by a BM during their very first watch. It is slightly rude, and for the innocent readers, or the innocent BM during their first watch, it is not referring to any of the actual tackles used by the Chief Bosun's Mate (the Buffer). The Buffer will have test weights and other equipment to ensure that their tackles are of sufficient quality to handle particular weights during an RAS or other seamanship evolution, but on this occasion, the reader is encouraged to say 'test tackle' quickly and then think of a lower area of the male body. The pipe is likely to raise a titter from many members of the ship's company.

It is also likely that at some stage the young sailor will be told to go and see the Buffer to ask for some green paint for the starboard navigation light.

Other sailors on their first day at sea have been told that one of their secondary duties was 'Indicator duty'. Noting that ships do not have indicators, the sailor would be required to run to the port or starboard sides and wave a flag to indicate that the ship was about to turn.

During one port visit, Daily Orders announced that 'when in Marseille tomorrow, rat guards will be required'. A young inexperienced sailor (AB Jones) asked what a rat guard was, and was asked by his leading hand, 'Have you never done Rat Guard duty?'

'Nooo,' said AB Jones.

Shortly after, the following pipe was made: **'AB Jones, report to the Small Arms Store!'** There he was provided with full combat gear and a night stick. He returned to his mess and said, 'How big are these bloody rats?'

'Massive,' said the Leading Hand, 'and whatever you do, do not let them near the ropes 'cos that's how they get onboard.'

For two hours AB Jones patrolled the jetty before the end of his 'duty'. He must have been a good rat guard[*] because he never saw one!

---

[*] Please note that a rat guard is a metal circle which prevents rats scuttling up a rope and into the ship. No sailors or rats were harmed in Marseille.

'Ted Rogers, dial 3-2-1.'
If you are unclear on the meaning of this, Google it!
'OM Let, Galley.'
'D'you hear there, the person holding the ship's ignition key, report to HQ1.'
There is no ignition key!
'RO Tate, Radar Office.'
This pipe is ordering Radio Operator (RO) Tate to report to the Radar Office. A radar, of course, *rotates* in order to provide a picture of surface or air contacts. It is unlikely that there will be a RO Tate onboard, hence this pipe is likely to be made in jest. There are, however, occasions when a person's surname may well have a close resemblance to an aspect of life onboard. Some examples:

Leading Supply Chain Specialist Pallett[*]
Petty Officer Missileman Gash (i.e. out all gash (see page 108)) – PO Gash spent his career telling people that his name was pronounced 'Gaysh'. Sadly, apparently he 'lost it' when he heard the pipe 'Out all Gaysh, Out all Gaysh'.
Chief Petty Officer Writer Inkpen
Naval Airman 'Screwy' Driver
Marine Engineering Mechanic Overal[†]
Chaplain Church
Petty Officer Writer 'Johnny' Cash
Master at Arms Sargent
Sergeant Sargent RM
Petty Officer Marine Engineering Artificer Funnell
Chef Baker
Medical Assistant Burns
Yeoman Bunting[‡]
Leading Chef Cook
Petty Officer (Cook) Cook
Chef Currie

---

[*] Stores usually arrive on a pallet.
[†] Stokers wear overalls.
[‡] Members of the Communications Branch were known as Bunting Tossers.

Engineering Technician Scott (i.e. ET Scott SCOT* Office)
Lieutenant Commander Anchor
Regulating Petty Officer Law
Leading Seaman Seaman
Petty Officer Steward Cioffi
Leading Seaman (Sonar) Ping
Engineering Technician (Marine Engineering) Tripp (known as 'Reset')
Chef Bacon
Writer Mailey
AB (Clearance Diver) Gee – Able Seaman Gee worked in a mine countermeasures squadron. His first names were Edward Francis, and as a clearance diver his name and title would have been: AB(CD) E F Gee.

Therefore: **'ABCDEF Gee, Gangway!'**

And perhaps the most infamous ghost pipe of them all …

On the occasion of HM warships crossing the Equator they are visited by King Neptune, whereupon all of those sailors who have never crossed the Equator (i.e. novices) are initiated into the ways of the deep King Neptune and his Queen accompanied by the Judge, the Judge's Clerk, the Doctor, the Barber, the Barber's Assistant, Lady Barber, Police, Safety Police, Bodyguards, Head Bear, Bears, the King's Messenger, Chariot Seahorses and the King's Trumpeter.† It should be noted that, whether a novice or not, some personnel will be re-inducted into the deep irrespective of their wishes; they are typically, the CO, XO, EWO, MAA, heads of department (despite, in my case, wearing a t-shirt from a previous deployment showing that we had gone across the Equator!).

The night before the ship reaches the Equator it will be visited by some of the King's representatives (the Bears) and his herald.

---

* SCOT is a long-range telecommunications system.
† They will bear a fair resemblance to some of the ship's senior rates.

Scene I – The Bridge
Time: 2000 the night before arriving at the Equator
OOW: 'The safeguard rule is now in force.'
Object bearing right ahead, Sir. Looks like some sort of fish. (Short pause). *Appears to be surfacing, Sir!*

Captain: *Very good! That will be King Neptune's herald. We are closing on the Equator rapidly. Executive Officer, pipe clear lower decks to the Forecastle. Guns, muster the Cadet's Guard. Officer of the Watch, stand by to ...*

(The Captain is interrupted by the lookout.)

Lookout: *Green One Zero, Sir, a light, near!*

Captain: *Very good, alter course towards it, Officer of the Watch.*

(Slight pause.)

OOW: *Stand by to receive boat transfer on the port side.*

Scene II – Both Herald and Captain speak through the main broadcast

Herald:
I've heard your ship's around,
Now tell me, whither bound?

Captain:
We sail from Singapore,
We've steamed for many a day,
Now I've got a lot to do,
So tell me, who are you?

---

* This particular *italicised text* (taking you to the pipe 'The Safeguard Rule is no longer in force' (page 53)) is direct dialogue between the Captain, the Herald and the OOW. Such dialogue in other circumstances would not be conveyed over the Ship's Main Broadcast, but on this occasion, for the purposes of drama and suspense, the interaction is acted out on the Main Broadcast for all to hear.

Herald:
I am the Herald of the court of his Oceanic Majesty;
King Neptune ordered me aboard and I'll commit no travesty.

Captain:
For you I'll stop my ship,
Come forth, and no more lip.

Look sharp, then, sire, if you please,
By what right do you challenge us on the high seas?

Herald:
By the custom of powers invested right,
In King Neptune and Queen Amphitrite
Who sent us to your mighty ship
To check and see if you are fit,
We cannot take you 'cross our line
Without the stamp of the Trident Sign.

Captain:
It is of course without disdain,
That I'll accept your word,
We're crossing into your domain,
So sheath that mighty sword.

Herald:
King Neptune will be glad, I'm sure,
To have you cross his border:
If you're a shellback, let us hope
Your papers are in order.

Captain:
A better tadpole never lived,
Or walked the ocean floor:
So tell King Neptune I've never crossed
His bloody line before.
And if you think I'm not so hard
Have Davy Jones inspect my guard.

Herald:
I'll do your will,
So, sound the still.

Davey Jones:
A frostier guard I've never seen
They look like hell and smell unclean.

Herald:
Before this mighty ship of war
Had slipped from her home port
A spy of mine had come aboard
Her complement to sort.
He's scanned the names of every one ...
Come forward now, your work is done.

The nominal list I've closely scanned,
To learn by whom this ship is manned.
1,000 persons more or less
Who by their conscience must confess
They have not joined our Royal Mess.
They must be made to taste the salt
Of my King's Royal Main.
And choke upon our pills and soap
'Ere they can cross again.

Herald:
At two bells of the forenoon watch
Tomorrow, come what may,
His Oceanic Majesty,
King Neptune will hold sway.
And by the ancient laws laid down
By custom will ordain
That all you tadpoles, young and old,
Be initiated in our name.

Captain:
Keep silence.

Assure King Neptune that we all
Are honoured by this meeting:
And please convey to him our thanks
And our most loyal greeting.
We shall be ready for our King

And glad to meet his Queen
And will she bring her daughters fair
To beautify the scene?

Envoy:
It cannot be: A sea nymph form
Would take each sailor's heart by storm.
Our good Queen spares them from such shows
Because they haven't any clothes ...
The Queen will come alone.

I command you all to rest with sorrow
The fittest will survive tomorrow ...

OOW: 'The safeguard rule is no longer in force.'

That evening, before the Bears and Envoy depart into the deep, they will pay a visit to each mess and hand the president or leading hand of each mess a list of novices who will be summoned as follows. It is likely that during the Bears' visit to each mess they might not receive a warm welcome, and some form of scuffling will take place. They will present the following summons:

NEPTUNE, by the Grace of Mythology
Lord of the Waters, Sovereign of all Oceans, Governor and
Lord High Admiral of the Bath,

Whereas it has pleased us to convene a court to beholden onboard His Majesty's Ship Prince of Wales on the upper deck thereof, at the hour of 0930.

By these presents We summon you, Lieutenant Claire Thompson, to appear at the said court to tender us the usual homage, and to be inducted into the mystic rites according to the ancient usages of Our Kingdom.

Here of nor you, nor any of you may fail, as you will answer at your peril, and to the delight of our trusty Bodyguards.

Given at our court on the Equator this 25 day of July in the year Two Thousand and Twenty Five of Our Watery Reign.

The ceremony takes place the following day on the ever-versatile flight deck, which consequently becomes the Court. The Court will be rigged with thrones, platforms, ducking stools and the ducking pool. At the appointed time the following pipe will be made: **'D'you hear there, clear lower deck of all personnel not on watch, muster at the Court of King Neptune.'**

Once the ship's company are mustered, the royal procession will begin, and the royal party will take its place in front of the assembled ship's company whereupon the King will make the following address:

> *My gallant Captain and Crew,*
> *Our pleasure's great at seeing you*
> *Once more on Our Equator.*
> *Old friends we notice by the score,*
> *But some, we've never met before.*
> *They'll be presented later.*

At this point the investitures commence. These will begin with the Captain and the XO/First Lieutenant. The investiture takes the form of the novice being placed on a chair precariously placed over a pool in which are placed the Surgeon, the Barber and Safety Police. At that point, prior to the novice being dunked into the pool, the Barber will gently massage a form of shaving foam upon the novice's face. Concurrently, a syringe containing all manner of goodness, and badness, will be placed into the mouth of the novice who is well advised to swallow the concoction. They are then dunked into the pool and are subjected to a small degree of violence from the Police.

From time to time it may come to the attention of the King's Intelligence Team that there is a shirker or a 'conchy' among them. The King will then proclaim:

> *It has been brought to our notice that Leading Electronic Warfare Kavanagh has not yet appeared before us. Police, arrest her!*

The defaulter will then be rounded up and initiated, potentially with a greater degree of attention from the Police.

Once all novices have been initiated, the ceremony will be complete, and novices will be presented with their royal certificate.

I was initiated twice into King Neptune's Kingdom. Crossing the Line has survived as a tradition in the Royal Navy and, although perhaps not as robust as it used to be in keeping with the times, it remains a unique moment, not simply because of physically crossing the Equator, but as an opportunity to boost morale at a moment that is likely to be quite some way into a ship's or submarine's deployment. I remember the contents of the syringe and I am ashamed to say that I spat them out. For that I was given a second helping by Charge Chief Price.

And to finish:

'This is the DCO. The fire in the Captain's cabin has now been extinguished. The fire was caused by a defective television. A smoke clearance plan has been enacted, and a sentry has been posted. Sentry is Able Seaman George. Personnel are to keep clear of the vicinity of the 01 Delta. End of exercise, end of exercise, return and stow all gear. There will be a debrief for the SSEP in the junior rates' dining hall at 0915. That is all.'

This pipe is welcomed by everyone onboard. Very few people like FIREXs, and the phrase 'end of exercise' indicates that life can get back to normal. Throughout the ship, for the next hour, people will hear the sound of breathing apparatus being refilled and tested, with the associated sound of whistles from the equipment.

And that is it, the final pipe. Many long pipes, such as this, will be signed off by the phrase 'that is all'. So, that is, literally, all. Carry on!

Acknowledgements

Many of the officers, sailors, Marines, Pongos* and Crabs with whom I served appeared in my mind when recalling these pipes and the associated memories and dits. Special thanks go to shipmates who contributed to this book, and hopefully I have recalled their contributions faithfully and with minimal embellishment. Many of them responded to my initial pipes on social media by adding their own recollections and dits, and some of those dits have been incorporated, so I cannot say this is all my own work (but you are not getting any royalties, I'm afraid). So to Knocker White, TDRN, Pete Simmo Simpson, Julie Looly Palmer, Amy Glover, Danny Glover, Neil Pedlar Palmer, Steve Dainton, Michael Cochrane, Mick Harris, Jenny Morton, Gary Lewis, Kenners, Toby, Will Blackett, Al Thomas, WO(MEM) Whisky Walker, Sarah Bearcroft, Andy Rhodes, Alan Nairn, Monty Mountford, Daz Knowles, Ian Stretton, Dr Phil Grove and, of course, Jim (for the amazing illustrations), thank you, and for anyone I have missed, please accept my apologies! As I wrote these pipes and recollections, and read those dits from people who engaged on social media, I would smile and very often laugh out loud. I hope you have too.

Thank you to Jude who helped me at a key moment of my time in the RN.

Thank you to my Mum without whom none I would not have been able to have had the opportunities I had.

Finally, thanks to all of those who encouraged me to write this book, especially my wife, Claire, and my sons, Tristan and Tom. And not forgetting Scrumpy.

---

* Members of the British Army.

Glossary

ABBREVIATIONS

AB	Able Rating
AER	After Engine Room
AIB	Admiralty Interview Board
BM	Bosun's Mate, usually an Able Rate
BRNC	Britannia Naval College, Dartmouth
CANMAN	canteen manager
CBRNDC	Chemical, Biological, Radiation, Nuclear, Damage Control
CDT	Compulsory Drug Testing Team
CO	Commanding Officer
CORRO	Correspondence Officer
CPO	Chief Petty Officer
CPOWTR	Chief Petty Officer Writer (senior pay and administration clerk)
CTH	'Call the Hands' (pipe)
CTP	cocktail party
CW	Commission Worthy; used to describe candidates considered worthy of promotion to officer
DCO	Damage Control Officer
DF	Deterrent Force
DO	divisional officer
DWEO	Deputy Weapon Engineering Officer
EDC	electronic distribution centre
EW	Electronic Warfare
EWO	Executive Warrant Officer
FIREX	fire exercise
FOST	Flag Officer Sea Training; members of FOST are known as FOSTies
LMA	Leading Medical Assistant
LO	Logistics Officer
LOA	Local Overseas Allowance, an allowance granted to naval personnel for runs ashore
MA	Medical Assistant

GLOSSARY

MAA	Master at Arms
MCO	Main Communication Office
ME	Marine Engineer (or stoker)
MEO	Marine Engineering Officer
MO	Medical Officer
MOD	Ministry of Defence
NAAFI	Navy, Army and Air Force Institute
NPFS	Naval Personnel and Family Services (not in current usage)
OOD	Officer of the Day
2OOD	Second Officer of the Day (under training to become an OOD)
OOW	Officer of the Watch, a junior Warfare Officer on the Bridge
Ops	The Operations Officer
OST	Operational Sea Training
PLR	permanent loan record
PMO	Principal Medical Officer
PO	Petty Officer
POMA	Petty Officer Medical Assistant
POWTR	Petty Officer Writer (senior pay and administration clerk)
PTI	Physical Training Instructor (also known as 'Clubz')
PWO	Principal Warfare Officer, usually a lieutenant commander Warfare Officer
PWO(A)	Principal Warfare Officer (Above Water)
QM	Quartermaster, usually a leading hand
RAS	replenishment (i.e. refuelling/reprovisioning) at sea
RF	Response Force
RFA	Royal Fleet Auxiliary
Rig	uniform
RN	Royal Navy
RNA	Royal Naval Association
RNFT	Royal Navy Fitness Test
RNST	Royal Navy Swimming Test
RO	Radio Operator
RPO	Regulating Petty Officer
S&S	Supply and Secretariat
SCC	Ship's Control Centre
SD	Special Duties Officer (an officer promoted from the Ratings Corps)

SOC	System Operator Check
SLt	Sub-Lieutenant
SRE	Ship's Radio Entertainment, a rudimentary organic radio station
SSD	Special Sea Dutymen
SSEP	Standing Sea Emergency Party
SUY	Senior Upperyardman
UDS	Upper Deck Sentry
UY	Upperyardman
WAFU	Wet and Flaming Useless, or Weapon and Fuel User (Ship's Flight personnel)
WE	Weapon Engineer
WEO	Weapon Engineering Officer
WO	Warrant Officer
XO	Executive Officer (Second in Command, often known as the First Lieutenant)

NAVAL EXPRESSIONS AND SLANG TERMS

adrift	late
Bish	Chaplain
bulkhead	wall
Bunting Tosser	member of the Communications Branch
Clubz	short for Clubswinger; nickname for the Physical Training Instructor
Dabber	Warfare Officer or Rating
dhobey	shower; also laundry (as a verb, to launder, or clean)
dhobey kit	washbag (slang)
dhobeyman	laundryman
dit	story (slang)
Dockie	civilian dockyard worker (slang)
dog robbers	jacket and tie
Dogs, the	a Watch from 1600 to 1800, or 1800 to 2000
draft, on	reassignment from one ship to another
evolution	ceremony or exercise
flat	an area of internal deck
gash	rubbish waste
Gib	Gibraltar
gizzits	souvenirs or memorabilia (for example of a shore run, or a sailor's time onboard)

GLOSSARY

goffas	fizzy drinks
Greenie	Weapon Engineer
Guzz	HM Naval Base Devonport, Plymouth
Hand	sailor
heads	toilets
ice cream suit	tropical white uniform
ickies	foreign currency
in it	asleep, in bed
Jack Dusty	Supply Chain Specialist
Joss	Master at Arms
Middy	midshipman (slang)
nutty	confectionary
oggies	pasties
oppo	opposite number/shipmate
Ops	nickname for the Operations Officer
planters	casual shirt and trousers
Pompey	HM Naval Base, Portsmouth
puns	punishment
Pusser	Ship's Logistics Officer, or often used to describe the RN in general
Reggie	Regulator (Police)
Schoolie	Education Officer
scran	lunch, dinner, breakfast
searider	FOST instructor/assessor on an exercise
sitrep	situation report (an update)
tabbing	smoking (smokers are known as tabbers)
turn to	work
uckers	Board Game based on Ludo
Writer	member of clerical staff
Yardie	Senior Upperyardman or Upperyardman, an officer promoted from the Ratings Corps

Index

AB (Able Seaman) 21
Action Messing 54, 55, 56, 81
Action Stations 53–54, 57
Admiral visits 113–115, 122
AER (After Engine Room) 42
AIB (Admiralty Interview Board) 32–33, 110
ammunitioning 23
amphibious assault ships 96
AOG (Aircraft on Ground) 69
Attack Party 42, 43

barbers and haircuts 35
bathing at sea 96–97
bathrooms and washbasins 13–14
BFPO (British Forces Post Office) 33
blockages in the sewage treatment system 64–65
BM (Bosun's Mate) 13, 18, 30, 48, 82, 85, 115, 125, 126
Bridge 26, 48, 50, 79–80, 88–89, 95, 115, 125, 129
British Army 57, 74, 76, 92
BRNC (Britannia Naval College), Dartmouth 13, 36, 37, 47, 76, 84, 95, 97, 99
Bunting Tosser 59, 127

CANMAN (canteen manager) 56, 81, 103–104, 124
Cape Wrath firing range 93
Captain (CO) 17, 21, 23, 24, 25, 27, 33, 48, 52, 56, 59–60, 61, 64, 71, 74, 75, 76, 79–80, 82, 84, 86, 88, 90–92, 98, 104, 110, 111, 113, 115, 118, 120, 128, 129–131, 133, 134
Captain's Secretary 34
car permits for dockyards 22–23
casualties 56, 57, 79

catering and dining 22, 54–56, 62, 63, 80, 111–112, 118
CBRNDC (Chemical, Biological, Radiation, Nuclear, Damage Control) States 51, 99–101
CDT (Compulsory Drug Team) 120–121
Ceremony of Colours 15–18, 28
Ceremony of Sunset (Evening Colours) 15, 17, 119, 120
charitable endeavours 112–113
Chief Bosun's Mate 83, 126
chillcons 110–111
church services 71–73
cleaning 13, 19, 45, 49, 63, 84, 85, 108, 113: of uniforms and clothing 73, 75, 84
cleansing station 100, 108
clothing and uniforms 28, 35–38, 47, 50, 73–75, 76, 81, 84
Communications Rating 17, 18, 27
Containment Party 42
CORRO (Correspondence Officer) 34
CPO (Chief Petty Officer) 26, 76, 77, 81, 84
CPOWTR (Chief Petty Officer Writer) 26, 63, 102
CTP (cocktail party) 116–120
CW candidates 105, 116

Daily Editorials 31–34, 35, 65
Daily Orders 15, 17, 40, 67–68, 76, 109, 126
Daily Words 67, 68
Dartmoor Training Area 72, 73
DCO (Damage Control Officer) 43, 44, 52, 134
Defence Watches 53, 112

INDEX

DEPCO (Departmental Coordinator) 71
DF (Deterrent Force) 29, 31
dhobey shack 75
dhobeying and dhobeymen 73, 75, 76, 104, 105, 116
DIMPS terminal 33
Direct Graduate Entry Officers 37
discipline and punishment 20–21, 121, 123
DO (Divisional Officer) 20, 21, 39
dockyard access 22–23
drug testing 120–121
Duty PO (Petty Officer) 29, 30
Duty WE Senior Rate 92
DWEO (Deputy Weapon Engineering Officer) 109

EDCs (electronic distribution centres) 13, 26
Electronic Warfare Ratings 46, 51
EMC (Extra Messing Charge) 111
EMCON (emission control status) plan 45
entertainment 81–82, 83
EWO (Executive Warrant Officer) 30, 53, 55, 120, 128
external telephone calls 88–90

Falkland Islands war (1982) 92, 107
FDO (Flight Deck Officer) 71
Fearnought suits 43
Fire and Emergency Party 19
fire outbreaks 42–44, 99, 119
FIREX (fire exercise) 27–28, 44, 48, 134
flight deck 9, 19, 52, 61, 67, 77–78, 80, 81, 83, 104, 107, 110, 116, 132
FOD (Foreign Object Damage) 71
foreign currency exchange 102–103
FOST (Flag Officer Sea Training) 44, 45, 49, 52, 53, 55, 72
Fridge and Freezer 110

Galley 27, 44, 54, 62, 68, 99, 112
Gangway 27, 28, 90, 107, 110, 116, 118, 125
Gibraltar 28, 41, 82, 83, 101–102, 113
graduate and cadet entry officers 37
Gully Gully Man 36
gunnery drills 92–93
Gunnery/Missile Ratings 92

Hands to Bathe 96–98
heads and bathrooms 63–64, 84
helicopters 69, 78, 80, 104
Herald of King Neptune 129–131
Herbert Lott awards 31, 43
HMNB Devonport, Plymouth 9, 30, 32, 122
HMNB Portsmouth 41, 122
HMS *Collingwood*, Fareham 28
HQ1 27, 30, 43, 44, 90

intruders 29–31

Jack Blair retail clothing 35–36, 38
Jack Dusties 38, 46, 47, 55, 59, 69
junior ratings 19, 47, 49, 50, 76, 96

keys 25–26
Killick Chef 27

Larne Target 93
Leading Steward 59
Leading Writer 21, 22
leak stopping 99–100
Liaison Officer 118
LMA (Leading Medical Assistant) 57
LO (Logistics Officer) 38, 55, 56, 59, 60, 75, 87, 88, 103, 110, 111
LOA (Local Overseas Allowance) 103
Longcast 88

MAA (Master at Arms) 10, 20, 125, 128
mail and correspondence 33–34, 69

MCO (Main Communication Office) 33, 88–89
MEO (Marine Engineering Officer) 46, 60, 75, 82
messdecks 72, 79, 84, 85
MO (medical doctor) 57, 60, 79
MOBs (man overboard exercises) 94–95
Movements Signal 24

NAMET (Naval Maths and English Test) 19, 66
Naval College Entry Officers 37
Navigation Officer 38
newspapers 31–33
NGLO (Naval Gunfire Liaison Officer) 93
novice initiation investiture at the Equator 128, 133–134
NPFS (Naval Personnel and Family Services) 82

OASIS computer system 65, 124
OOD (Officer of the Day) 10, 17–18, 19, 23, 24–27, 28, 30, 31, 44, 75: and 2OOD 28, 29
OOW (Officer of the Watch) 13, 14, 48, 61, 67, 80, 95, 125, 129, 132
Operations (Ops) Room 46, 50
Ops (Operations Officer) 88, 89
OST (Operational Sea Training) 13, 43, 44, 49, 51, 52, 81, 84, 85, 99, 109: under FOST supervision 49–51
OUTs (officers under training) 116, 119

PAS boats 105, 106, 107
Pay 2000 114
Physical Training Instructor (Clubz) 56, 66–67, 68, 78, 108, 125
PLR (permanent loan record) 38
PO (Petty Officer) 104
PO Caterer 110, 111
PO Steward 118
PO Writer 101, 102, 103
POMA (Petty Officer Medical Assistant) 57
port visits 104–105
'postcard/haircut' runs 34–35
Preparatory Pennant 17, 18
'prewet' evolution 100
provisions and 'store ship' 109–111
PWO (Principal Warfare Officer) 45, 46, 51, 54
PWO(A) (Principal Warfare Officer (Above Water)) 92

QM (Quartermaster) 13, 18, 19, 30, 48, 67, 75, 80, 106, 115, 121, 125
quarterdeck 14, 29, 81, 93, 107, 108

RAF 7, 57, 71, 74, 76
RAS (replenishment at sea) 40, 41, 58–59, 85, 94, 97, 126
Ratings 30, 40, 46, 92, 119
Regulating Office 10, 19, 20, 108, 122, 123, 124
RF (Response Force) 29, 30
RFA (Royal Fleet Auxiliary) 58
RNFT (Royal Navy Fitness Test) 67
RNST (Royal Navy Swimming Test) 97
RO (Radio Operator) 20, 79, 127
Royal Artillery 93
Royal Marines 76, 92, 97, 93, 120
RPO (Regulating Petty Officer) 85

saluting standards 25, 76–77, 107, 119
SCC (Ship's Control Centre) 21–22, 27, 48, 124
seasickness 62
Seawolf missile launchers 92
Sharkwatch 96–97
Shiphaz Board 26, 27, 29, 96
ships: HMS *Argyll* 52; HMS *Aurora* 79; HMS *Chatham* 46, 55, 87; HMS *Endurance* 75;

HMS *Newcastle* 28; HMS *Nottingham* 26, 101; HMS *Somerset* 9, 52, 72
Ship's Office 115
ship's programme 60–61
shore leave 21, 22, 28, 105, 121–122
'shouting' (pipe) 42
SIB (Special Investigation Branch) 72
Signals Board 24, 33
slang terms 7–8, 19, 22, 31, 35, 41, 47: dits 7–8, 11, 84; flat 56; gash 108
Small Arms Store 124, 126
smoke alarms 41–43
SOCs (System Operator Checks) 45, 46
SOTV (Ship Open to Visitors) 104
SOW (Swimmer of the Watch) 94–95
sports 77–78
SRE (Ship's Radio Entertainment) 47
S&S (supply and Secretariat) officer 34
SSDs (Special Sea Dutymen) 40, 41, 67
SSEP (Standing Sea Emergency Party) 63–64, 134
Standard Fleet Time 63, 64
station leave 122
'store ship' 109–111
submarines 33, 67, 77, 100
Supply Chain Specialist 31
Support Party 42, 43
SUY (Senior Upperyardmen) 37
swimming aptitudes 97–98

Thursday War 49, 50, 51, 53
time checks 45–46

toilet roll 87–88
training 73, 85, 99, 100: HMS *Raleigh* training establishment 9, 75, 76, 84, 97, 99

UDS (Upper Deck Sentry) 29–30
University Cadet Entry Officers 37
upper deck 23–24, 28, 40, 41, 46, 67, 92, 100, 110

Visit Liaison Team 104–105

WAFUs (Ship's Flight personnel) 47, 52, 62, 69–71, 74, 81, 122
Wardroom 104, 106, 108, 116, 119, 120
Warfare department 19
Warfare Officer 31, 116
Warfare Ratings 30, 40
Watch and Station Bill 40, 41, 50
Watchkeeping Certification 34
WE (Weapon Engineer) 30, 31, 40, 47, 62, 85, 92, 122
WE Senior Rate 92, 121
WEO (Weapon Engineering Officer) 46, 60, 91
White Ensign 15, 18, 119
Whole Ship Watch 40
Williamson Turn 95
Writers 20, 21, 115

XO (Executive Officer/First Lieutenant) 17, 21, 25, 44, 47, 59, 79, 82, 83, 85, 96, 98, 113, 115, 116, 118, 120, 124, 128, 129, 133

YOFB (Young Officer Fleetboard) 24

ABOUT THE AUTHOR
Richard Harris served for 31 years in the Royal Navy; joining the RN Reserve as an able seaman, and leaving the Regular Service as a Commodore in 2023. He served at sea in nine ships and undertook operational deployments to the Arabian Gulf, South Atlantic, Mediterranean and Arctic Circle. He commanded the RN New Entry Training Establishment, HMS *Raleigh*, as well as being responsible for training Officer Cadets at Britannia Royal Naval College, Dartmouth.